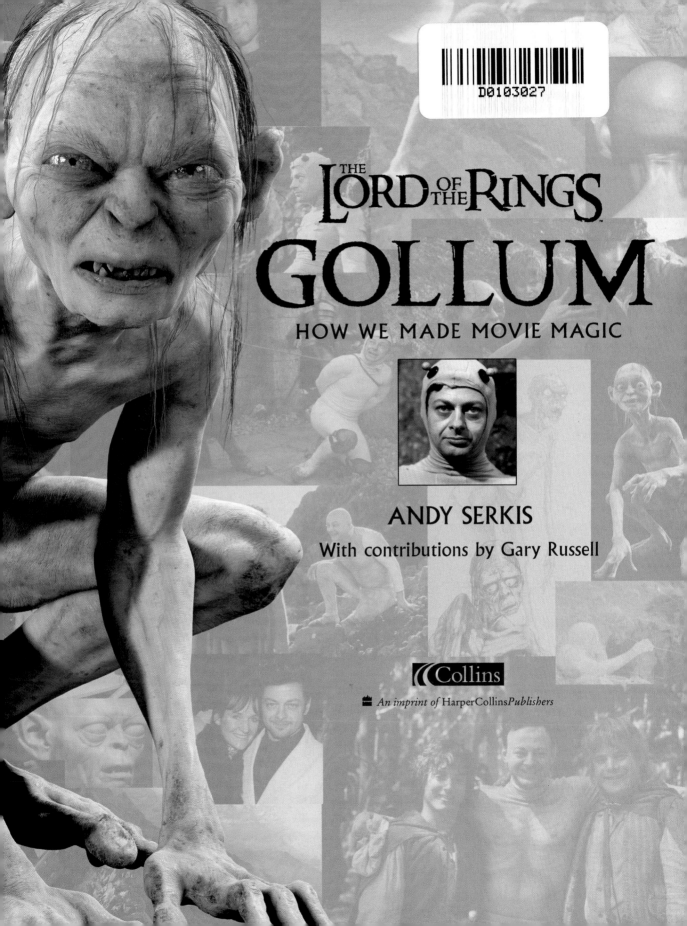

THE LORD OF THE RINGS
GOLLUM
HOW WE MADE MOVIE MAGIC

ANDY SERKIS

With contributions by Gary Russell

Collins

An imprint of HarperCollinsPublishers

Contents

INTRODUCTION
To begin at the beginning...

I am on my way to New Zealand to finish post-production on *The Return of the King*, well into the fifth year of being involved in this almighty mountain of a movie, and I'm seriously worried that the vivid memories I thought would never leave me are beginning to melt into prehistory and personal legend. I'm sure that certain events already exaggerate themselves in my mind while others are fading gently away.

I had wanted to chronicle the journey of creating the on-screen character of Gollum, because from the moment I started to try to unravel him, I could sense that this was going to be a very unusual acting challenge. I'm not really that partial to reading actors' memoirs, as they often tend to be rather self-elevating and you feel you 'had to be there'. But one day, during a motion-capture session for *The Two Towers*, Fran Walsh, who became one of the most important figures in the evolution of the character, inspired me to put finger to laptop and tell my side of the tale. It dawned on me that the world had changed dramatically since we had all started work on the films in 1999 and that everyone's perceptions about Gollum were changing as the years went by.

This account of taking Tolkien's Gollum out of his books and on to the screen is for the most part my personal story, focusing on an actor's journey and experiences. It goes without saying that Gollum was created by an army of immensely talented artists, animators, technicians, fellow actors, great screenwriters and a genius of a director, and they all have their own perspectives on bringing such a wonderful creation of literature to life. These are touched upon by the contributions to this book, courtesy of interviewer Gary Russell. But be assured, everyone who worked on Gollum could write their own story. With cinema's increasing usage of computer-generated technology to create creatures and characters, this book celebrates the pioneering work of making 'him' truly life-like. I have had the privilege of working with the world's greatest in their fields, and have made wonderful friends, and Gollum belongs to us all.

See you on Mount Doom ... my preciousss!

Andy Serkis
JUNE 2003

CHAPTER ONE
'It's mine. My own. It came to me!'

The January sun was out over Hackney, East London, and doing a grand job of distracting my anxiety as I waited by the phone. The day before, I had auditioned for the part of Bill Sykes in Alan Bleasedale's new adaptation of Dickens' *Oliver Twist*. It was a role that I felt I was 'destined to play', but I knew I'd completely screwed up the audition and wanted to try and get back in for another go. I was feeling as murderous as Sykes himself. The phone rang, I pelted into the kitchen, scattering our three cats to the four winds.

'Hello?'

'Oh, hi Andy, it's Michael Duff. Now, I don't know if this will be of any interest to you, it's a bit of a strange one.'

'Oh yes?'

'Yeah, the Hubbards are casting this film of *The Lord of the Rings*, which starts shooting in New Zealand in the autumn.'

'Oh really?'

'Yeah, now the thing is, well, I'm not entirely sure what they mean by this, but they want to see you for the voice for an animated character which would probably be about three weeks' work.'

'Oh... right.' The enthusiasm drained out of my voice. *Typical*, I thought to myself in best self-persecuting actor mode. *Aren't there any proper acting roles on offer? I mean, there must be loads of characters in it.*

'Have you read the book?' Michael asked. 'Apparently the world is divided into those that have and those that are going to.'

'No,' I said, exposing my ignorance of great literature, then adding rather pathetically,

'I did read *The Hobbit* when I was at school.'

'Right, well, the character they want to see you for is Gollum.'

Gollum... *Gollum*. The name conjured a dim and distant memory of sitting on a 273 bus, aged about eight, on the way to school, and reading a book with a dragon on the front, and some image of a cave with a bedraggled slimy ghoul in it.

In the middle of my reverie, the front door opened and in came Lorraine, my partner (now wife), with our four-month-old daughter, Ruby.

'Any news?' she said, unhooking shopping bags from the handles of the baby buggy where Ruby lay sleeping.

'Well, Michael's just rung and—'

'Oh yes?'

'I've got an audition, but it's just for the voice, of this character Gollum in *The Lord of*—'

'Oh wow! Andy, that's brilliant!'

'Have you read it?' I asked, rather over-defensively,

'Course I have, it's amazing, and Gollum! He's a great character, he's trying to get the Ring, and you feel so sorry for him, and he calls it something... my... my 'precious', and... You *must* have read it?'

'Well... no. I mean... I did read *The Hobbit* when I was at school.'

'Oh Andy, you've *got* to go for it!'

So that was how it all started... just like that, out of the blue.

I had a few days to prepare. In fact I then got recalled for the Bill Sykes audition, and so within one week I had the potential opportunity of playing two incredible roles from English literature.

I needed to work fast, as I didn't have anywhere near the level of understanding for Gollum as I did for Sykes. I'm a slow reader at the best of times, but having just entered the realms of parenthood, and discovering that lack of sleep turned me into

a sloth and the merest glance at reading matter would make me collapse into unshakeable slumbers, I knew that I would never be able to get through enough of The *Rings* in the time allotted. I therefore focused on the back history of the character, which is beautifully and compassionately explained to Frodo by Gandalf in the early chapter 'The Shadow of the Past'. It is here that we learn how Gollum was once a Hobbit (of the Stoor kind) who killed his cousin for the Ring and was ousted from his society because of the effect that the Ring had on him, turning him into a malicious thief. He was shunned so he crawled into the Misty Mountains, becoming progressively lonely, haunted, and a mad, gurgling sound emanated from his mouth.

I started to work on his voice. How should he sound? I could hear it, but I couldn't do it. It sounded cartoony when I tried reading the script pages I had been sent for the audition. That was because I was plucking at straws, just doing random creature voices. I needed to root it somehow, find a psychological basis, an emotional truth. What exactly has the Ring done to him? Why is he so full of pain and self-pity? Why does he mutter and babble to himself? I started to think about where he would physically carry his pain, and decided that his throat could be deeply affected, constricted by subconscious guilt associated with killing Déagol, so that when he talked he felt like he was choking.

And just then, whilst I was sitting there in my kitchen trying to imagine how this would actually work, one of our cats, Diz, tripped in and started his usual routine of coughing up fur-balls. For anyone who hasn't witnessed a cat doing this, I'll briefly explain. The cat licks itself to get clean, but inevitably a lot of loose fur gets swallowed, which then collects in the back of the throat to the point where the cat starts to cough. This cough becomes a convulsion − making the entire spine ripple in an attempt to eject the mass of furry sick − accompanied by an unearthly wheezing, until finally it comes out of the cat's wide open jaw, and splats on to your kitchen floor. *Voila!* Fur-balls.

Initially, I got up to clear up the mess thinking, *Do you really have to do this now? I'm trying to create art here.* But later in bed, not able to sleep, I had one of my rare moments of revelation, which felt akin to St Paul on the road to Damascus or Archimedes in his bath. (I nearly always do my best work in bed at night, gripped by the fear that I'll never be able to play a part.) My heart started racing. *Maybe he sounds like a cat being sick! Maybe when he says*

Gollum, understandably, was the most difficult character to conceive of. A fundamental problem in our design work on The Lord of the Rings *was that we were trying to capture the essence of everyone else's preconceived idea of what Middle-earth and its inhabitants should look like, because they've read the book a hundred times. You don't want to step away from people's individual perceptions, because Tolkien described everything so incredibly well, particularly in the case of Gollum, who is almost iconic. Yet, we wanted to add our own essence to it, and Peter Jackson's vision. So it was essential that we captured exactly what people conceive Gollum to be but with our own subtle twists and turns. As a result, most people who saw our designs said that he was exactly how they imagined Gollum to be.*

Richard Taylor, Weta Workshop Supervisor

'Gollum, Gollum,' it's like an involuntary convulsion, like coughing up fur-balls.

I quietly tried it out, careful not to wake Lorraine in case she thought I really had lost the plot. It wasn't entirely successful, because I was lying down and all I seemed to be doing was giving myself severe neck strain, so I decided to wait until morning when I could physically crouch down and convulse properly.

My first thoughts of how this film would be made, I have to admit, were that it was just going to be some kind of huge special effects-fest where you get a director who isn't interested in actors, an unsayable script, lots of shots of things which look totally unbelievable, characters you couldn't give a monkey's about, and a deeply unfunny gimmicky computer-generated CG sidekick that you can't understand. It seemed to be a far cry from the kind of film and television that I was interested in: socially relevant drama, with powerful characters, facing titanic struggles in living day to day. So, as I was deciding what on earth to wear for this Gollum audition, I was secretly thinking to myself, *I'm never gonna get this, and it'll probably be a load of crap anyway* (a common pre-audition mabtra employed to toughen one's skin in case of rejection, and make one feel more in control of one's destiny).

However, when I met casting director John Hubbard and he explained the authenticity Peter Jackson sought in bringing Tolkien's book to the screen, I got excited again. I remembered that Peter had directed *Heavenly Creatures,* which I'd thought was a sublime, dark and wonderful film. John then showed me some of Alan Lee's incredible illustrations, including some of Gollum, and by the time we were set up to shoot me on tape to send to Peter in New Zealand, I was really fired up. I climbed on to a chair, tucking one knee under my backside, and hunched my shoulders over into a low stoop, so that I could look up at the camera. The audition scene was an early draft of the moment in Emyn Muil where Gollum swears on the 'precious'. John called 'Action!' – and out came this weird, choking cat-sicky voice.

The thing was, I had to fully act out the pain and wretchedness, and the manipulation, in order for the voice to work. I just couldn't do it any other way. I could feel my face contorting into bizarre expressions. In the middle of the take I looked up at John, who was being Frodo and Sam, and his face was a picture of pure shock. So when he called *cut*, I wasn't quite sure if I'd completely blown it. There was a brief pause, and then John's shock melted into a big smile. I remember him saying, 'Andy, how do you do that?' He was incredibly complimentary, and I'm deeply grateful to him for enthusing me and being responsible for beginning this journey for me.

The tape was Fed-Exed to New Zealand, and time went by. By all accounts, they tested the voice against an early animation of Gollum, and weirdly enough I somehow bore a strange resemblance to him and the voice seemed to fit. The next thing I heard was that Peter Jackson and his screenwriter partner, Fran Walsh, were coming to London in April 1999 to cast some of the roles and wanted to see me.

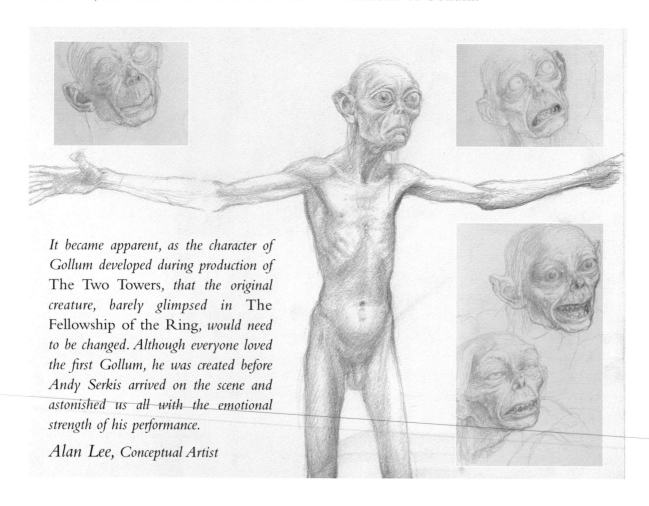

The meeting was to be at the American church, Tottenham Court Road. I cycled into town, muttering in Gollumese, trying to get my head back into the place I'd been a couple of months before. I had already had some good feedback from the first audition, so I was feeling fairly positive about things. Also, I had started filming *Oliver Twist* and as any actor will tell you, confidence is always greater when you're working.

John and his assistant Amy MacLean were there to greet me, and they said, 'You'll have a great time, they are so delightful.' I walked in, and there were Peter and Fran.

Now, I do not say this lightly, but there are few people in this world that you genuinely feel an affinity with when you first meet them, but I felt it as soon as I laid my eyes on them. They had an extraordinary energy, warmth and passion that was intoxicating, and the conversation we had about *The Lord of the Rings* had me totally enraptured. They opened a huge portfolio of conceptual artists' sketches and I sat marvelling at this world that they were about to create. They talked with such great authority and clarity about the characters, and finally Peter explained how he wanted to approach the character of Gollum.

It became apparent, as the character of Gollum developed during production of The Two Towers, *that the original creature, barely glimpsed in* The Fellowship of the Ring, *would need to be changed. Although everyone loved the first Gollum, he was created before Andy Serkis arrived on the scene and astonished us all with the emotional strength of his performance.*

Alan Lee, *Conceptual Artist*

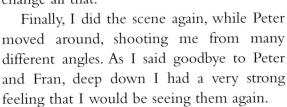

They had decided to make Gollum a totally CG (computer-generated) creature from very early on in pre-production. They had felt it would be impossible to cast any actor, even with prosthetic make-up, because of the extreme physical appearance, nature and demands of the role. However, the job of the actor who got the part would not simply be putting a voice on top of an animated creature. In tune with the levels of authenticity they were setting out to achieve, they were adamant that Gollum would have to be able to act alongside whoever was cast as Frodo and Sam. It would seem ludicrous to have two actors having to react to a tennis ball on a stick. The complex nature of Gollum's psychology and the level of interaction in the scenes would mean that an actor would have to be there on set to emotionally drive the acting decisions. The 'in the moment' acting choices would then be organic between all three characters, and then the Gollum audio performance would become a guide track for the animators to work from.

Although Peter wasn't quite sure exactly how this would work on the floor, whether the actor would be delivering the lines sat down on set or from behind the camera, he knew he wanted to make Gollum the most emotionally truthful, complex and interactive CG character that had been seen in a live action film. There was also a mention of experimenting with the use of motion capture, sticking dots on your body and tracking movements, even putting dots on your face. I had no idea what he was talking about – at that stage, I didn't know the difference between blue screen, green screen,

any-colour-you-like screen, let alone motion capture. This meeting, however, was going to change all that.

Finally, I did the scene again, while Peter moved around, shooting me from many different angles. As I said goodbye to Peter and Fran, deep down I had a very strong feeling that I would be seeing them again.

Barandoff Studios in Prague were built in the 1930s to facilitate the production of Hitler's Third Reich propaganda movies, like Leni Reifenstahl's infamous *Triumph of the Will*. The place has a very strange, cold, utilitarian feeling, so it felt odd to be filming Dickens here. We were nearly at the end of four months shooting *Oliver Twist*, and were filming the murder of Nancy when I got a message from my agent that call had come through. I had finally been offered the part of Gollum and would be required to start filming in September.

I returned to London to find a large package, which I tore open like a three-year-old on his birthday, to find three fat scripts for a film called 'JAMBOREE – An affectionate coming-of-age drama set in the New Zealand boy scout movement during the years of turmoil, 1958-63'.

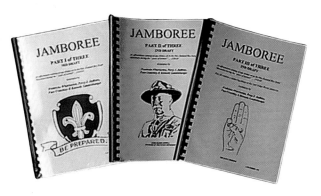

We wanted Gollum to be a really special character. I always felt that having a performer in some sort of suit or prosthetics just wouldn't give Gollum quite the unique quality that we felt that he needed. I am a bit wary of CG characters and I thought that the only way that Gollum was going to work was to try and let a human being drive it as much as possible, and I was very protective of Andy's performance. You can have ten people animating in a department, and no matter what you do with the character, you've still got ten interpretations from each of those animators sprinkled round the movie. So Gollum would have had this slightly manufactured feel if we went that way.

We had to animate Gollum in some shots where he does things that no human could possibly do, like climbing down rock faces, but largely what we did was let Andy develop the character on set during the fourteen months that we were shooting the film. He was filmed doing all of the action as Gollum, walking on all fours, jumping around, doing all the dialogue, and so creating an entire character, just as any actor would. After doing several takes with Andy, it wasn't too hard for Elijah Wood and Sean Astin to visualise what Andy was doing after we removed him. Andy would then do the voice for them off camera, and ultimately we put in a CG version of Gollum, but one that captured everything that Andy gave to that role.

Peter Jackson, Director

I don't remember having a conversation with anybody about a boy scout movie.

I turned the pages to find the opening titles of the three *The Lord of the Rings* films: *The Fellowship of the Ring, The Two Towers* and *The Return of the King*. Strange people, I thought. It wasn't until I got to New Zealand, and saw location signs with 'JAMBOREE' on them, that I realised it was an elaborate code of secrecy to protect the filming and prevent the script from falling into the hands of those hungry to make a quick buck. But, I'm jumping ahead of myself. It was going to take slightly longer for me to get to New Zealand than I thought.

My mind was set on going out in September and so the next few weeks were quite frantic, trying to sort things out before the big trip. We moved house, Lorraine was filming her TV series, *Playing the Field,* up in Leeds, I started preparing for Gollum, my contract was being finalised, then suddenly September arrived and... nothing. Everything went quiet. I had heard that other actors had gone out to start rehearsals, and yet here I was, like a cat on a hot tin roof, raring to go, not knowing what was going on. And then I got the news from producer Barrie Osborne – the schedule had been changed and I wasn't going to start until after Christmas. I couldn't believe it. It was like being picked to climb Everest, and then told you had to wait at base camp!

I took the role of John Thelwall, the real-life eighteenth century Jacobin revolutionary, in Julian Temple's film *Pandaemonium,* which centred on the life of Samuel Coleridge, and was filming in North Devon. The country-side was beautiful, and Lorraine came down with Ruby to visit, but what should have been a weekend of bliss ended up with us terrifying the locals with one of the biggest, ugliest rows we've ever had. A few days later, Lorraine rang to tell me that we were going to have another baby!

The point of this diversion is really that if I'd gone out to start filming *Rings* when planned, my little boy wouldn't be here today. So thanks, Barrie, and production, I owe you one!

Christmas came and went, Y2K arrived and the world didn't stop turning, and *The Fellowship of the Ring* was building up a head of steam. I was again delayed in going out to start filming, and as each week went by I wondered if it was ever going to happen. I started work on *Shiner,* a boxing film starring Michael Caine, in which I played his over-eager, self-important minder. In between takes I'd secretly run back to my trailer and read *Rings*, trying to build up a picture and

profile of who Gollum was. Then, at last, my marching orders came through, and I was definitely going to be heading out in April. So I pulled Gollum off the back burner, and applied some serious heat to the melting pot as I searched for the character's psyche.

Like many of the people in *The Lord of the Rings*, Gollum, as an archetypal character, can be mined from a rich seam that runs through mythology and literature, art and cinema. From the Bible Lucifer the fallen angel, and we have the stroy of Cain and Abel, in which Cain murders his brother out of jealousy and is cursed – 'You will be a restless wanderer on earth'.

In the Icelandic saga *The Volundarkvitha,* the ring of the protagonist Volund falls into the hands of a pirate called Sote, who becomes obsessed by it, to the point where he buries himself in a deep grave mound and patrols the tunnels, sword in hand, a crazed insomniac, paranoid that someone will steal his ring.

Gollum could be related to Shakespeare's misshapen earthy slave Caliban in *The Tempest*, Charles Dickens' obsequious Uriah Heep in *David Copperfield,* or to Victor Hugo's tortured and reviled Hunchback of Notre Dame. He can be traced to a line of monsters trapped within human form, with complex and terrifying split personalities, including Dr Jekyll and Mr Hyde, the werewolf, Frankenstein and Dracula, all of whom have become icons of cinema.

I turned to works by painters such as Otto Dix, Egon Schiele, Francis Bacon, Lucien Freud and fantasy artist Brom (top right) for inspiration. These artists had all painted

characters in physical and psychological pain, and their brushstrokes reflected a tangible sense of torment that I could really connect with. In particular, I remembered being haunted as a child by the painting 'The death of Saint Jerome' by Leonardo da Vinci. The memory of the anguish on his face and his semi-naked, ageing body jumped back at me and became part of the physical vocabulary.

I received a package of research material from New Zealand, including some photos of

Peter displaying a range of facial poses with sculptures of Gollum's face mimicking his emotions – creepy, angry, hurt. These were early facial models and were to change drastically over the years." At this point in time he looked quite like an alien: bald with huge eyes.

There were also sketches by the incredible Alan Lee and John Howe. One pencil sketch by the latter, which to me depicted Gollum as a cross between a homeless junkie and a survivor of a concentration camp, directly influenced how I would move as Gollum in the films. From this image (overleaf) I strongly felt that Gollum should be on all fours at all times, that the weight of the addiction to the Ring had reduced him to a crawling wretch. It just seemed wrong that he could walk on two feet – his descent into madness was like the evolution of man in reverse.

It has to be said that the most important clue to my interpretation of the character came from Tolkien's books. Crucially, before he

'I think it is a sad story,' said the wizard, 'and it might have happened to others, even to some other Hobbits I have known.'

11

At one point, it seemed like everyone was doing Gollums. Poor Gollum was one of the hardest creatures to pin down, thin, wiry and slippery as he was.

John Howe, Conceptual Artist

degenerated into the creature, Gollum was Sméagol and came from a wealthy Stoor Hobbit family. Stoors inhabited regions near to water, where they could fish. The race was a matriarchy, and the head of his family was his grandmother. He was a curious Hobbit, interested 'in roots and beginnings'. He was 'downward looking'. One could imagine that things might have been very different, had the Ring not crossed his path. This was a key thing to remember when setting out on the road to play him. As long as I could hold on to that, I could believe he was redeemable.

The starting point for me was finding a metaphor for the Ring. I thought that part of Gollum's dramatic function as a character,

was to represent what the Ring does to an individual so that the reader of the book, or the watcher of the film, feels like this could happen to them. If Frodo is an everyman, then in a way so is Gollum. He represents an someone who is flawed, in his case deeply. But what would be the point of portraying him as purely Machiavellian, or evil? Where would the connection be for the audience? Thinking about it, everyone on the planet is flawed – I know I certainly am anyway. Stick me in a traffic jam when I'm late and I become a probably certifiable potential murderer – for a second anyway – but put me in my garden with my children and I can be as peace-loving as Gandhi!

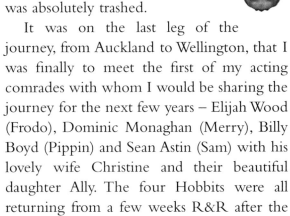

'The Ring left him'

Gollum's sense of loss, betrayal and rejection also drives his obsession. I began to imagine the Ring as a lover who had left an abusive relationship. Gollum's pain is like that of a wounded, psychotically jealous husband whose wife has left him, and who imagines a million ways to get revenge.

How could the Ring physically and mentally torture him, age him, yet keep alive his fierce loathing of himself and the world? I needed to find a tangible metaphor for the Ring's power over him. And then I realised that the concept of addiction could be the key.

With nothing more than a huge bundle of vague notions and images floating around my head, I was feeling like I couldn't really progress any further without discussions with Peter and Fran, when suddenly that time arrived.

5 April 2000

Saying goodbye was awful. We had not slept well and the prospect of being away from Lorraine and Ruby for an unknown length of time was really daunting. But the time had finally come, and there were tears as I climbed into the car that was taking me to the airport.

At that stage of my life, the prospect of getting on a plane and flying for over 24 hours seemed unthinkable, even though I'm pretty well travelled. I was definitely a first-time long-hauler, because as everyone else settled down to sleep, I was feverishly reading and re-reading my scripts, until I was ridiculously over-stimulated. My nervous energy and excitement about the job I was about to embark on meant that I was like a live wire. By the time the plane touched down in Auckland, I was absolutely trashed.

It was on the last leg of the journey, from Auckland to Wellington, that I was finally to meet the first of my acting comrades with whom I would be sharing the journey for the next few years – Elijah Wood (Frodo), Dominic Monaghan (Merry), Billy Boyd (Pippin) and Sean Astin (Sam) with his lovely wife Christine and their beautiful daughter Ally. The four Hobbits were all returning from a few weeks R&R after the first block of filming, and we spotted each other as we boarded the plane. They were clearly already a team with a history, and they regaled me with amazing stories of filming during the first six months.

As the plane descends into Wellington, you fly over a stretch of water that separates the North and South Island, known as the Cook Straits, through which very strong winds can blow, all the way up from the Antarctic. My first experience of a 'mild southerly' had me clenching my armrests for dear life, almost turning me religious to prevent a sea landing!

CHAPTER TWO
Welcome to planet Middle-earth

There's no doubt about it, it's strange flying to the opposite side of the world and there being no acute culture shock on arrival. Wellington is a very welcoming place, with its waterfront, café culture, retro and modern shops, deco houses alongside steel and glass modernism, and the stunning national museum, Te Papa Tongarewa. It's a compact, hip city nestled into hills and bays.

No, the real culture shock comes from being taken by car into the suburb of Miramar, down Stone Street, and turning right into a disused paint factory that is now Middle-earth.

Imagine it: you are delirious with jet-lag, but your heart is pounding with excitement. You get out of your car, there's around a hundred terrifying looking Orcs eating their lunch, trying to fork Thai noodles into their prosthetically extended mouths (some not very successfully, I might add) and you're nearly run over by a huge section of 'Mordor rocky outcrop' which is being moved by truck. You go straight through a studio, into Rivendell, and on to wardrobe where there are row upon row of Gondorian Rangers costumes. You strip down to your undies, are fitted in a skin-tight suit, someone pulls a hood with no eye-holes over your head so you can't see, and then a voice says, 'Hey Andy, can I introduce you to

Barrie Osborne, the producer?'

'Hi Andy, how y'doin? Welcome.'

'Hi,' you reply from the darkness, extending your hand into nowhere.

No time to stop, it's straight over to Weta Workshop, where you are greeted by its high priest, Richard Taylor, who's talking to you while listening to five other people in his earpiece. You're given a tour of the workshop by Hannah Bianchini, who guides you through this wondrous world (and explains that a 'weta' is an ancient and *very large* New Zealand insect that is virtually indestructible). This place is a goldmine of creativity. Sculptures and models of cave trolls and Balrogs, the Argonath, the watcher in the water, Elvish and Orc armour, weapons that are all individually handcrafted, chainmail made ring by ring, Hobbit feet and ears moulded by the hundred. Upstairs you go, trying to absorb this wonderland as you are whisked past storyboards and conceptual artists' paintings showing all the environments, huge 'miniature' models of Isengard and Helm's Deep, a Mûmak, and on you go. You could spend days here, marvelling at the sheer amount of mind-blowing artistic output. And all the time the passion and energy coming out of the people who create it is quite staggering.

The thing that I always fought against with Gollum was that he had such big eyes and such a little nose, which, to most people, means 'cute'. I was trying to get that craftiness and that smartness in my designs, and the fact that, despite his seemingly harmless look, he could strangle anybody if he got his hands on them! I think I was giving a bit of age to him – although sometimes he still had a child-like quality, particularly when eating fish that he knows he shouldn't be! I went for a less skeletal look than a lot of other designers, as well. I did a number of quick sketches to show facial expressions – none of which were very relevant, but they were still fun to draw! We thought a lot about what, if anything, Gollum would wear. I did a couple of ideas, some with a loincloth while another sees him with a sort of well-worn shirt. I liked the idea of it still having pockets and showing varying degrees of wear and tear. For the scenes where his two personalities asserted themselves, I was just trying to bring a bit of the characters up. The conflict between Sméagol and Gollum – you can imagine the frustration that he would feel at those times where he 'crosses over' and Sméagol remembers Gollum and Gollum remembers Sméagol and there's all this confusion and pain. I think the fantastic thing about this project has been the fact that we have had so much time to develop characters, and the philosophy seemed to be – with the design – not to spend too much time putting gloss into the illustration but have the shapes right, the shape of the face or size of the body.

Warren Mahy, Designer / Sculptor, Weta Workshop

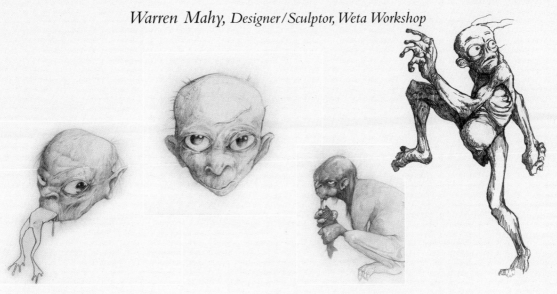

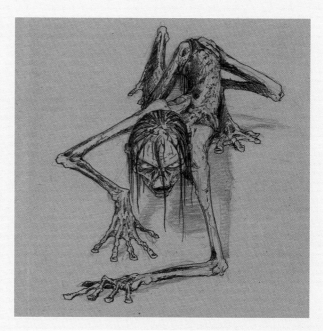

It was decided that a skeletal nose was a little bit too zombie-like. We determined early on that it was probably necessary to give him a human nose, otherwise he becomes too unsympathetic. Also, he's got that bloated pot-belly look, something that was introduced in a design which Warren did, and so we pursued that idea for a short while – thinking that he'd have a tiny little gut, because obviously he doesn't eat very much but when he does it all swells up – but the idea didn't get very far.

For quite some time, nobody had started looking at the colour scheme on

Gollum, so I thought I would. I reasoned that his skin, while once flesh toned, had now changed. He's been out in the wilds a long time so it's almost like grass stains have worn into him from running around in the dirt, and there's very little of the actual flesh colour left. Again, this probably has the effect of making him a little bit too 'monstery'. The final design we went with actually had a very pale flesh tone, rather than with any green hues.

Daniel Falconer
Designer / Sculptor, Weta Workshop

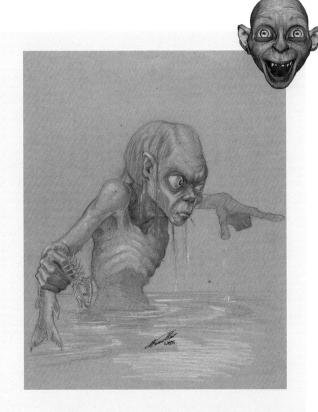

The idea of designing Gollum was a massive challenge but I relished taking it on, because everyone who has ever read the books has thought about him, everyone has a preconceived idea of what he should look like. Therefore actually realising the guy is incredibly difficult. And I think in that respect all the Weta designers were keen to have a go and get our ideas out there because, obviously, we all, as readers of the books as well, had differing views on what he looked like. The thing that is cool about him is that that he's probably the most tragic character in all the books. Tolkien doesn't write people's thoughts in his books, it's old saga-style, but you do get inside Gollum's head because he talks to himself. He's the only character where you see his thought processes working; I think that draws you to him as well.

As an artist, what epitomises Gollum for me is big toes, big spindly fingers and big eyes. As with an earlier sketch of mine, I imagined him as malnourished – too thin perhaps, but still dangerous. You can imagine him in earlier times still in reasonably fertile lands, surrounded by plenty of birds' nests, plenty of young rabbits, and so on. So at one time in his life, he was probably quite well-fed, sneaking around Elven forests, just spying on people because that's what he'd do. Later, of course, when he hasn't eaten for days, and he won't eat the Elven food, he's quite thin and drawn. That's a very strong impression I took from the books, that towards the end it's sheer force of will that's keeping Gollum alive, as clinically he's probably dead!

Ben Wootten
Designer/Sculptor, Weta Workshop

Then, when I thought I couldn't take in anymore, there he was – Gollum, sculpted in clay, in several incarnations, looking up at me with his huge eyes. There was even a full-size, naked, maquette, the sculpture that would be scanned into the computers to create the digital template for the character. Already, there was a huge amount of detail: his back had been lacerated with deep scars from the torture he'd received, and his bones were practically poking through his pale greenish flesh.

My mind started to race, weighing up how he looked, versus my ideas built up over the last year about how he should look. I stopped listening to the voices around me, my hands went clammy, and at that precise moment I had the first dawning realisation that, unlike any character I'd ever played before, one of the major challenges would be the fact that I didn't totally 'own' the role.

Actors work in a myriad of different ways but acting is essentially a selfish craft. I'm not talking about over-inflated egos and delusions of grandeur (that goes without saying!) – I mean that it is fundamental for an actor playing a part that he or she must feel they embody, understand, know that character's soul, and that they 'are' that person more than anyone else on earth. (Whether anybody else agrees with their interpretation is a different kettle of fish.) For instance, if you are playing Hamlet, and in the first week of rehearsal the actor playing the gravedigger comes up to you and says, 'If I was playing Hamlet, I'd give him a big red welt around his

neck from a suicide attempt, to show how utterly desperate he is,' you'd probably say something like, 'Yeah, great idea, I'll think about that.' But really you'd be thinking, *Go away you nosey old fool and concentrate on how to dig graves.* Then you'd avoid him for the rest of rehearsals. Debate and collaboration helps to firm up your own opinion, but finally you've just got to suck it up from the core of your own guts, otherwise, well, forget it! You can't stand up on stage in front of a thousand people, thinking, *I bet they all know who Hamlet is better than me, but I'll have a little go anyway.* You have to believe, *I AM HAMLET!*

I AM GOLLUM! Well actually, Andy, you're a part of Gollum. You're the voice and emotions (and eventually the movements), but the body will be taken care of by many very talented people, with their own equally valid opinions. Your body will vanish into thin air and be replaced by digital ones and zeros, so get your head around that.

'*Go in,*' as Gollum says at the entrance to Shelob's Lair, '*or Go back.*'

'Andy, are you OK or do you want to go back to the hotel?'

I shake myself out of my jet-lag induced nightmare. Daydream. Day-mare.

'Huh, sorry, no I'm fine, let's carry on.'

'OK, now we're going to Weta Digital.'

From the clay dust, polystyrene, latex and airbrush paint fumes of the workshop, we step through a door into the pristine, air-conditioned nerve centre of pixel world, where finally my mind is completely blown away. I'm led into the small conference room, where I'm introduced to the visual effects team and some of the animators. Enter Randy Cook, director of animation. I'm shown a single test shot of some Gollum animation, which looks incredible, even though it's still in its infancy (a scene from Cirith Ungol, with Gollum, Frodo and Sam on a ledge, which had been shot at short notice before I'd arrived as wet weather had closed in while filming near Queenstown, so this was shot as 'cover').

After a good night's sleep and breakfast at Fidel's on Cuba Mall, I headed down to the Wellington Performing Arts Centre, where production had arranged for me to use a dance studio. My first day was devoted to experimenting with Gollum's physical vocabulary.

I had spent a great deal of time going through the books, listing Tolkien's boundless descriptions of the different ways 'he' travels. He is variously described as climbing 'as if he were a spider', like a 'grasshopper', a 'frog', a 'puppy fawning over his master', with 'feet slapping on rocks', and 'turning his head back on his scrawny neck'. Tolkien obviously delighted in building up the physical and vocal imagery of this dysfunctional, wandering wretch, and for an actor trying to embody him, this is a rich feast.

Towards evening, I was picked up from the hotel by the trilogy's co-screenwriter Philippa Boyens and taken out to the Helm's Deep location. As we arrived the sun was just setting. The gargantuan set loomed over us and everyone was getting ready for another unrelenting night of battle. They had been filming Helm's Deep for nearly four months and were exhausted. It was almost a separate movie all of its own.

I met Orlando Bloom (Legolas) coming out of his trailer, brimming with an almost insane energy that you'd imagine vampires to have before a night out on the town. And finally, a year after our initial meeting in London, which seemed a lifetime ago, I saw Pete. Here was a man clearly on a mission of Herculean proportions, and seeing

him in action confirmed my growing admiration for this great leader. He welcomed me warmly and introduced me to the crew (or, more precisely, one of the crews – at any given time during principal photography there were up to seven units filming simultaneously all over the North and South Islands). It was beginning to feel like I was truly onboard.

The rain was horizontal the next day as I drove around the bay to Pete's house to work with Fran and Philippa on the script. It was early days, and at that point they'd been working flat out on *Fellowship*, so this was the

first venture into Gollum-world since the early drafts. We talked generally about Gollum's background, the relationship with Frodo and Sam and how the Ring 'affects you according to your moral stature'. It was clear that they were a formidable writing team and had evolved a way of combining great storytelling structure along with a freedom to explore characters. We all agreed that the metaphor of addiction was useful for the obsessive, craven, lustful nature of Gollum's behaviour.

The drive up to Tongariro National Park takes around four to five hours. I shared the journey on 10 April with Elijah and we spent some time starting to get to know each other. Also travelling with us was Janine Abery, Barrie's assistant, who was to become a great friend. (Janine and Tanya, who also worked with Barrie, were the patient, caring and devoted friends, and touchstones of the cast. They worked and played hard, and we all adored them.)

I had been a huge fan of Elijah's work, particularly in *The Ice Storm,* and was so excited to be working with him. He has an incredible depth and understanding of life that completely belies his young years, and I was to find out on set that his energy, focus and consummate professionalism really gave power to all around him. He just *was* Frodo. We started to tentatively unravel the Frodo/Gollum relationship, and by doing that began to show each other what we were about.

We were on our way to Mordor – true to film form, the first scenes we'd be shooting together would be the climactic moments of

their storyline. And then we saw our hotel in the far distance – the Grand Château, perched on its own under the gigantic, recently active volcano, Mount Ruapehu. The 1920s hotel, which reminded us all of the hotel in *The Shining,* was our home for the next few weeks. Every evening we'd all gather together in the hotel's cinema, have a beer and snacks and watch what everybody had been doing during the previous day's shooting. A lot of film directors hate actors and non-essential personnel to watch the 'dailies' or 'rushes', but this was just one example of the feeling instilled by Peter that we were *all* filmmakers trying to create this story together. It was almost like watching your own family in home movies.

Finding my feet

I am a hair kind of actor. Some actors find an external key to their character is the type of shoes they wear, others what they've got in their pockets, but for me it's hair. I wanted to feel the wind against my skull, like Gollum, to feel more vulnerable, brutal and dehumanised. The Nazis shaved the heads of prisoners in labour camps to erase identity, and as I wanted Sméagol to have lost his identity, I shaved my head. (It had the added benefit of meaning I didn't have to wear the hood with eye-holes, which along with the skin-tight suit made me feel like the gimp from *Pulp Fiction!*)

I was preparing for the fact that I would never get the normal stimulation one gets from having costume and make-up to assist me in the characterisation.

I climbed on to the Weta special effects make-up bus, which was located in the car park of the Whakapapa (pronounced 'Fackapapa') ski slope. I asked if I could try wearing a pair of Hobbit feet to continue work on Gollum's movement. After all, he was a Hobbit once, and although his body had become emaciated, the bones in his feet would still be the same size, and his toes would have evolved to be more powerful and claw-like as he crawled and climbed on all fours.

I was convinced they were thinking *Who is this strange person?* as I sat down to be fitted with a pair of second-hand Sam Gamgee feet.

'But isn't Gollum going to be CG, and aren't you just doing the voice?' If I had a pound for every time someone on the crew said that to me in the early days, I'd be a rich man. *Well,* I wanted to explain, *you see I'm playing him on set, and so I'm going to be acting him, doing the voice, yes, but I can only do the voice if I'm in character, and I can only do that if I know the character, and knowing the character means embodying him, which means being inside his head, his skin, his bones.* But instead I just replied, 'Yes, I am just doing the voice,' and let them think I was a bit strange.

Eventually I got my feet, and took myself off to some rocks, where I could move around on the real terrain. After a few hours of isolation, with the mist rolling around me, I started to feel closer to 'him', which was a good job, because the following day I would be shooting my first scene.

That night I didn't sleep. Too nervous. So I got up while it was still dark, put on my head torch and went jogging down the track to Tawhai Falls and spent a couple of hours 'getting into character'. Then I crawled all the way back down the track (about half a kilometre) until I got close to the hotel. Someone spotted me, so I ever-so-casually stood up and walked past him and got some coffee from the restaurant. He must have thought I was severely deranged!

I was crouching in my trailer, in my 'gimp' suit, waiting to go on set. Trying to stay focused, in character, tense as a coiled spring. I felt Gollum's blood flowing through my veins, I was ready to do it, right there and then. An hour went by, *come on… come on…* And another, and another. Eventually word came, 'Andy, sorry, we're not going to get to you today' I nearly imploded, it felt like I'd been holding my breath for hours, 'but Randy Cook is here and would love to shoot some reference footage for

animation.' In came Randy, with John Shields, fellow animator, and a video camera. And we went off to a small rocky outcrop and I let off steam as they filmed Gollum in his natural habitat.

Madness and addiction

Lust. Pure, craven, animal lust. The quickening of the heart, the blood vessels making the eyes heavy with anticipation, the drying in the mouth, the excruciating moment of heightened desire, to the point of intense agony. *I really need that bar of chocolate.* And then the glorious release, the golden feeling of light flowing through your veins, the pure ecstasy of the rush, the feeling of really being alive, momentarily all-powerful.

I figured we have all, at some time in our lives felt these physical symptoms when we are suddenly caught up in moments of uncontrollable lust, or intense desire

for something, (or indeed someone). It seemed logical to take this idea of lust to a very dangerous, psychotic level. Gollum is, in my opinion, dealing with a level of obsession and addiction that most people thankfully don't ever have to face. But what's the point in trying to find an un-actable notion of the Ring's power? Acting is about connecting the audience to an emotion, feeling, or concept, so I wanted to bring this lust into an area of understanding that people could empathise with.

As we know, addiction takes on many forms in our society. Food, tobacco, alcohol, these things make us feel better about ourselves, unless they control us and then we begin to 'love and hate them, as we love and hate ourselves'. Anorexia, bulimia, nicotine addiction and alcoholism eat away at our mental and physical core and eventually dominate us, so we think we cannot exist without them. We deny there's a problem, becoming pathological liars and cheats to feed the addiction. The cycle is very hard, sometimes impossible, to break.

What if you were addicted to shoplifting, gambling, drugs? Or to violence, crime, or murder? Imagine only feeling satisfied, calm and at rest by killing? So instead of having to rush out and buy a packet of cigarettes because you were desperate, you had to assault and kill someone. How much would you 'love and hate' yourself then?

Gollum is a mess. He is controlled by an obsession, a 'heavy burden' that only a Ring-bearer understands. Over the course of their journey he shares this with the one person who understands him, and in return Frodo connects with the addictive Gollum because he is beginning to feel the power of the obsession growing in him.

Without wanting exclude any of the audience, who hopefully will connect with Gollum's instabilities, I'm focusing specifically on the idea of Gollum being a drug addict. He's a Ring junkie. His mind, body and soul is driven by the desire for his fix from the 'precious'. He is tormented psychologically and physically, as if he is going through cold turkey. He feels sick, wasted, jittery, anxious, and will go to any lengths to get his fix. He's become a paranoid schizophrenic, a self-serving, dangerous wreck with delusions of grandeur. Gollum is in the Ring's thrall forever, in his own hell on Middle-earth.

I know a number of people who are battling with addiction of different kinds, and I am always amazed at the experiences they have had, the madness they have endured, and the bravery with which they face each day. I also know that in different circumstances, my own personality could have allowed me to be led down a different fork in the road of life. As I get to know Gollum I feel a strong sense of 'there, but for the grace of God go I.'

13 April 2000

I was driven along a one-way rocky track to a ski-lift, which then silently carried me up to another track that led up to the set, a rocky ridge with breathtaking views overlooking Tongariro and Mount Ngaurahoe. We were shooting Scene 256, in which Gollum leads Frodo and Sam out of Emyn Muil. It's the shot in *The Two Towers* where Gollum crawls ahead up a rocky gully and calls back to the Hobbits, and at last they're out of the rocky maze, revealing a panoramic vista over the Dead Marshes.

I was escorted on to set to work with this unit for the first time. The pressure was on. I knew that the expectation for the character was phenomenal. For many fans Gollum is a favourite, and I knew the crew would be dying to see how he was going to be played.

People's jaws dropped. Who the hell is this? And what in the name of J.R.R. Tolkien is he wearing? I could see people sniggering out of the corner of their mouths and laughing silently to each other. Believe me, meeting a crew of around a hundred hard-assed Kiwis halfway up the side of a volcano wearing what amounts to a homemade, tie-dyed fetish outfit just about borders on being one of the most embarrassing moments of my entire life. In the future, this 'costume' was to be dubbed a 'unitard', which I have to tell you describes exactly how I felt wearing it.

Anyway, I tried to blank out the hysteria going on around me, and then Pete arrived. I thought he would restore order, but he took one look at me and started giggling as well! Caro Cunningham, the first assistant director, came down harshly on the situation. 'Right, we're rehearsing, so everybody shut up or go away.'

Blimey, I thought to myself, *she doesn't muck about!* Pete gathered Elijah, Sean and me together to discuss the scene. This was the first Gollum shot (bar the wet weather shot mentioned earlier) and everyone was slightly flying by the seat of their pants − except me of course, because I wasn't wearing any. Pete's thinking was, basically:

1− We'd shoot the scene with me 'on camera', and Elijah and Sean as Frodo and Sam would act off what I was giving them. This would be known as a 'reference pass', i.e. reference for the visual effects department. A motion-controlled camera would be used so that the shot could be repeated exactly next time when we would...

2− Shoot the scene for real, with me off camera, delivering the dialogue from behind the camera with the same timing. Having encoded the performance in their minds, Elijah and Sean would then have to imagine I was still there, which is no easy thing to do (and in the hands of less focused actors could have been disastrous).

3− Finally, a 'clean pass' would be shot, with no actors at all, but the camera replicating the move to give a clean background 'plate' for animation.

There was nothing left to do but to try it out. The set was locked down and Caro called action.

I start thinking to myself as I crawl up the gully, *Master trusts us, yes 'precious', this way, yes, here we are.* Then I call out 'Hurry Hobbitses' as I reach the ridge. I point towards a huge blue-screen backdrop, Frodo overtakes me, then as Sam comes towards me I'm thinking, *But the other one hurts us, and we hates him,* and then I mumble, 'Nice Hobbit'.

'Aaaand CUT!'

At last, I was no longer a Gollum virgin. I had completed my first shot on *The Lord of the Rings.* Now, I wasn't sure what Pete was really expecting from me. At that early stage, I'm pretty certain he wasn't quite sure himself. He knew that he wanted an actor on set, but I don't think he was expecting a fully realised acting performance, which is what I was trying to give him, mainly because I couldn't do it any other way. But what I do know is that over the coming weeks, Peter saw that there was someone giving Gollum an emotional backbone, not just giving a vocal performance. Playing out the scenes physically blended with a 'conventional' acting

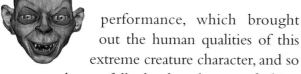

performance, which brought out the human qualities of this extreme creature character, and so he carefully developed a way of taking my 'on set' performance to another level.

Elijah and Sean were, I think, quite bemused, and I did think, *This must be totally bizarre for them. I mean, at least when I look up at them I see Frodo and Sam, and I just play off them, but when they look at me, all they must see is a man in a gimp suit, with a face that makes Jim Carrey's look relaxed and a voice that sounds like a cat being sick.* I had total admiration for the fact that they could act with me. It wasn't an easy ride for any of us to begin with but gradually we hit our stride together, and between us, we eventually eliminated the technical hurdles and concentrated on the drama of the scenes.

The very first time I saw myself on screen during rushes I wanted to crawl under a rock and never come out again. It was just too weird. There were Frodo and Sam walking through the blasted rocky landscape of Mordor, everything working perfectly to create a magical reality, then suddenly this bald lunatic in pale green spandex comes lolloping into view. It was like a very bad nightmare, like a Dalí painting gone wrong. I felt like everyone in the cinema was looking at me, I was finding it hard to swallow. *Get me out of here!*

CHAPTER THREE
Another world

I love working. I hate being on standby.

I was on standby. I had been on standby for a while. There are two ways of dealing with it.

1– You sit in your trailer, in costume, for hours, going nuts, and then you don't work.

2– You go off with a mobile phone for a few hours to see some of Tongariro National Park.

Mark Ashton, second assistant director *extraordinaire*, was a prophet and could accurately predict which would be appropriate for the day. There was a period of time when I was on standby for days.

I am, by nature, a keen 'outdoor kinda guy', and I've spent a lot of time in mountain environments, climbing and walking with groups of people and on my own. To be dwarfed by nature always gives me a sense of connection and a feeling of being truly 'in the moment'. New Zealand wilderness really offers that possibility on a grand scale.

I started off by taking the Whakapapa forest walk, an easy circular route on the lower slopes of Ruapehu, which is a stunning tramp through luscious bush and pristine streams. I thought a great deal about Gollum's isolation and the time I spent on my own fed into this.

Next on my agenda was the Tongariro crossing – an amazing one-day tramp across volcanic plains, taking in the Emerald Lakes, ascending the perfectly formed volcano of Mount Ngauruhoe, past the red crater and up Mount Tongariro itself, and finally descending through podocarp forests. It is so true when they say 'New Zealand, home of Middle-earth', for I felt I had been to another time and place and been away for days on end.

While shooting in central North Island, Zane Weiner, veteran unit production manager, threw a party in Ohakune, a ski town south of Mount Ruapehu, which almost changed the economy of the region in one night! The evening was legendary, making its way into print in the local paper, the sceptics viewing it as a decadent, debauched example of 'what them film folk get up to'. I can't imagine why they would think such a thing… My strongest memory of the night was driving back to the Grand Château at about 3 a.m. and suddenly, miles from anywhere, coming across a large Maori family whose car was in flames. They were standing on the road, clutching their children and a few possessions. I called the fire brigade, and a little later Andy, the medic from the set, happened to be passing and together we took them to a hostel. Nobody was in so we just piled them all into the rooms and let them get some sleep.

Blue sky. The side of a volcano, 5000 feet up.

'And action!'

'We Hatesss Bagginsss.' I leap through the air, crunch on to rocks, jump on to Frodo, grapple, roll, roll, roll, strangle, strangle.

'Aaaaaaand cut. Stop… STOP. STOP!!!'

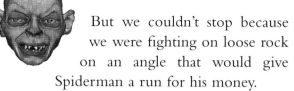

But we couldn't stop because we were fighting on loose rock on an angle that would give Spiderman a run for his money.

'OK, that's the reference pass, so Andy, you can step out for this one, Elijah we're on you.

Andy, if you can do the dialogue and call out the timing of the moves. Thank you. Final checks. And roll camera. Camera speed. Sound speed. Aaaand action!'

Andy as Gollum: 'We hatesss Bagginsss.'

Andy, shouting directions: 'Leaps through the air, landing, jumps on Frodo, grapples...'
What am I doing???

Andy and Randy go under the Misty Mountains

The next day, Randy Cook and I decided to head out to Waitomo glow-worm caves, a chance to get to know each other, talk Gollum, and do some 'cave research'. It was a stunning drive from Whakapapa to Waitomo, where we bravely donned wetsuits and large inner tubes, and threw ourselves into a black hole, which dropped into a subterranean river that flowed through the Ruakuri Cave.

It was a thrilling three-hour expedition, which totally transported us into another fabulous world. It was perfect as food for the emotional memory, as far as the Misty Mountains back-story was concerned, and in between fits of hysterical laughter as we dropped unexpectedly into plunge pools and marvelled at the tiny specks of light emitting from the glow-worms, I imagined Gollum slipping his invisible fingers around the neck of some unsuspecting quarry. It was a great day, nicely ended by listening to Louis Prima as we drove home.

20 April 2000

'It's my birthday, my love, and I wants it.'

But I wasn't going to get it, because I was on standby again. I was feeling pretty frustrated now, I was so full of Gollum I was bursting to let him out, but no, it's trailer limbo for you today, Serkis.

Birthdays are funny things, aren't they? I kind of love them and hate them. I was pretty certain that nobody knew that it was mine today, so I wallowed in a bit of private self-pity at being so far away from home in my trailer prison. Then I started thinking, *OK, so when he kills Déagol, is it really his birthday? Why does Tolkien make the day the 'precious' finds him his birthday? Or is it Gollum perpetuating his own lie to gain sympathy? And is everything that Gandalf reports to Frodo the real truth or just his version?* After obsessing for hours, I was fortunately released to go and do some reference footage with Randy. We worked on an early version of a scene that demonstrated the Gollum/Sméagol personality split, so the animators could start thinking about how the physiognomy would change between them.

Then, to my complete surprise, Janine presented me with an enormous birthday

you how much their on-screen role bled into their off-screen persona. It just happened. Billy and Dom were inseparable, Elijah and Sean felt like brothers. Also, one has to take into account that we were all spread to the four corners of Middle-earth, with seven units filming at least three separate storylines over two islands. I would never act with Ian McKellen (Gandalf), Brad Dourif (Gríma Wormtongue), Christopher Lee (Saruman), Viggo Mortensen (Aragorn), Liv Tyler (Arwen), Miranda Otto (Éowyn), Orlando Bloom (Legolas), John Rhys-Davies (Gimli/Treebeard) or Sean Bean (Boromir).

cake in the production office, and that night we had a party... of which I have no memory whatsoever.

It was coming up to the Easter break, and most people were heading back to Wellington. Not me. I had decided to opt for the wilderness.

I was feeling a genuine sense of loneliness, which was both a good and a bad thing. Good because Gollum is a deeply lonely creature, but bad because I felt that the other cast members had all bonded through their roles – they were the Fellowship or the Hobbits and I was this weird unknown quantity which people didn't really know how to deal with. It wasn't that people were unfriendly – far from it – I just felt slightly outside of the acting fraternity, and I'm sure that it was as much me keeping myself to myself. Talk to any actor who worked on these films and they will tell

Anyway, I had decided to soak myself in Gollum's anger and self-loathing on my own for an extended period of time, so I took myself off to the Wanganui River. I intended to canoe on this remote river for an afternoon and then find a batch or home-stay, work on the script and commune with nature. It was a few hours drive to Whakahoro, the chosen starting point for my waterborne adventure.

The moral of the story is, as any boy scout would know, '*Be prepared*'. I, of course, wasn't. As I hauled my canoe on to the trailer to take it to the water's edge, I noticed another couple of canoeists were packing a lot of gear and food into barrels and strapping them on to their vessels. The man who had rented me the canoe asked if I needed a spray skirt, which I declined, thinking, *Spray skirts are for wimps, and anyway I'm only going for a couple of hours. So what if I get a bit wet? Big deal!* I was so wrong. He explained that it was a

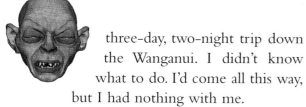

three-day, two-night trip down the Wanganui. I didn't know what to do. I'd come all this way, but I had nothing with me.

'Well do you want to go or not?' he asked.

'I haven't got any food or camping equipment,' I replied.

'Not a problem, just help yourself to anything in the freezer and grab some veggies out of the garden,' he kindly offered.

Being a vegetarian, the freezer full of lamb chops was no good to me, but I found a few pieces of bread and a jar of Vegemite in a cupboard, and then quickly grabbed a couple of tomatoes from the vegetable patch.

Next thing, I found myself sitting in my canoe, ready to push off from the shore. *What the hell am I doing?* I thought to myself. *Oh well, it'll be an adventure.* The man told me there were two campsites on the way, the second being a *marae* (a Maori reserve, on which stands a spiritual meeting house called a *whare*), and he gave me a photocopied map saying, 'I'll see you in Pipiriki in three days.'

I punted off and gently drifted downstream, excited and a bit cautious. I was going to be on my own in this canoe for three days! It was idyllic: blue sky, a huge canyon with overhanging lush forest, and the sound of water trickling down its vertical walls. I felt like Martin Sheen in *Apocalypse Now*. I paddled slowly for about half an hour and then the river took a slow turn to the right. Suddenly, a dead cow floated past me. In the distance there was faint rumbling sound.

What's that then? I thought. It got louder and louder... and then my heart started thumping and fear gripped me as I realised I was heading for what looked like rapids.

Within seconds I was being thrown all

over the place, smashing into rocks and tumbling backwards into plunge pools, but miraculously I managed not to capsize. Excited to be alive, I looked at the soggy photocopied map, and then wished I hadn't.

It was 97km to Pipiriki. There are 121 rapids between Whakahoro and Pipiriki. I had been psychologically scarred for life going through one, and I had 120 to go!

In fact I got the hang of it pretty quickly and even began to enjoy that rush of adrenaline you only get from trying to stay alive. It is the most beautiful and spiritual of rivers, and has a strong link with Maori history and legend. I slowly began to soak up its atmosphere.

As dusk approached, I found the campsite. Now 'campsite' to me means somewhere with hot showers and a little shop where you can buy a tin of baked beans, but this was basically the only, tiny piece of level landing area in the canyon, which had a spiral of smoke coming from a old fire. As darkness fell, with just the sound of the forest wildlife, with no tent, sleeping bag or even a torch, sitting there with nothing apart from waterlogged bread, Vegemite, a squashed tomato and my old battered copy of *The Lord of the Rings,* I realised it was going to be a long night.

And then, just when it was getting too dark to read, I heard the sound of voices coming from upstream, and lo and behold, four Wellington city councillors turned up in their canoes, and saved the day. Jonathan, Rory, John and Brendan shared their food and wine with me, even shared their tent. If I ever see them again I'll take them out for a meal at the swankiest place of their choice. They were amazed I was out there on my own without provisions, but they couldn't believe that they'd bumped into the person playing Gollum!

I woke at 5 a.m. and climbed back into my canoe. I had to cover some serious distance in order to reach Tieke Marae (about 60km). It had rained in the night and the water had risen and was much faster flowing, but I managed to negotiate all the rapids successfully. I was really enjoying this incredible wilderness and being able to plug into Gollum's isolation.

That evening I arrived at the marae. As a visitor (*manuhiri*) I was invited on shore by the welcoming call (*karanga*) of the marae's female host. We pressed noses (*hongi*) and I could then enter. It was an unforgettable evening. Everyone prepared food, ate and cleaned dishes together. Stories and songs were shared, and a *haka* (war chant) was performed by one of the young men. I felt very privileged to have experienced Maori culture in such a personal way in such an idyllic setting. I slept the night in a communal hut, and set off early the next morning.

The last leg of the journey was glorious, the river meandering gently as it worked its way south. The Maori motto for the Wanganui is 'I am the river and the river is me' and I was beginning to feel strangely connected to it myself, and as I approached my destination I was sad that this magical journey was ending. I felt as if I'd been away for months, and when I got back to the Powderhorn Hotel in Ohakune and phoned Lorraine, I kept repeating excitedly, 'It's OK, I'm fine, I'm back'.

Back in Morgul Vale, we were supposed to be shooting the opening scene of the Frodo, Sam and Gollum storyline for *The Return of the King* in which Gollum is trying to wake the Hobbits and hurry them up, but it snowed so we were trailer-bound for a while. Eventually the skies cleared and we got back to work.

The time was drawing near to leave the Central North Island and get back to Wellington to begin some studio work, but before I left I managed to spend a couple of more days up in the Tongariro mountains, one on the summit of Ruapehu itself, with its huge steaming crater lake, before driving west the next day and climbing the perfectly symmetrical cone-shaped mountain of Taranaki. According to the local myth, Taranaki was once part of the Tongariro range, but Tongariro caught Taranaki with Pihanga, his lover, a small volcano. He erupted with fury and so Taranaki fleed westwards, leaving a deep gorge in his wake, the Wanganui River. Maori people worried that the two volcanic lovers might one day get back together and so they didn't settle in the area between them.

I was beginning to feel homesick. I was starting to worry that I might not get back home for the birth of our second child, which was getting very close. And I was sick and tired of phone calls.

One night I sat in my room in the Powderhorn Hotel and wrote this poem for Ruby.

So many weeks have passed,
Since I
kissed your 'precious' forehead
goodbye.
In all that time
I've merely
crossed the planet,
climbed mountains,
ridden horses,
and canoed rivers,
seen the Milky Way
and sulphurous pools.
Whilst you,
my exquisite child
have seen the world
from the doorstep
and wondered,
and grown
and understood it profoundly
without needing to move an inch.

My darling Ruby,
every marvel that opens
up before my searching gaze
is dull compared
to the glistening thought of you
transforming day by day.

CHAPTER FOUR

Motion Capture

After the Easter break, I began for the first time to get a real sense of how all the separate Gollum departments worked together. Basically they can be divided into four different areas:

1– *On set performance*: recording positions and performance on 35mm film.

2– *Motion capture*: taking what the actor does physically and converting it, in real time, on to the computer generated Gollum model.

3– *ADR (Automated Dialogue Replacement)*: Laying down vocal tracks for the animators to work from.

4– *Animation*: developing and refining the character, frame by frame, using all the above as a touchstone for putting Gollum into the scenes with the other actors.

On 1 May 2000 I met the mocap (motion capture) team, in yet another converted studio space in Miramar. I was quite excited because I didn't really know what to expect.

Gollum's a creature that you couldn't really shoot in a rubber suit because he really has to interact. He's crazed yet he has these gentle moments to him, so he's almost human, a kind of emaciated ET-like creature. It just pushed us to the point where we realised we had to make this guy fully computer generated and yet ensure he looked absolutely real in his actions and the way he speaks. So we went for animation via motion capture and we actually had Andy Serkis do every motion possible.

Andy got right into the character, giving us more than we ever thought we would need, and we just had to scale it back down for this emaciated Gollum creature on screen. It was beyond amazing, and it enabled Gollum to be real. We didn't want people sitting there thinking Gollum was an amazing looking CG creature, we wanted them to believe he was real. We wanted to keep him moving around, just like a real actor, interacting fully with the other people.

Jim Rygiel, Visual Effects Designer

Enter Patrick Runyon, a large, softly spoken man who had previously worked with lions and other big cats, who ran the operation, with his team consisting of Ramon, a Mexican puppeteer, Greg, who'd worked in video games, and James (Moggey) and François, the computer whizzes.

In semi-darkness, they explained the process, which I learned is born out of the medical research industry and had filtered its way into the entertainment world, mainly through video games. Then I was off to be fitted into a specially designed black suit, covered in highly reflective referencing dots positioned by means of velcro at strategic points wherever your body bends or has extremities.

I was led on to a small podium, surrounded by lights and cameras. Standing

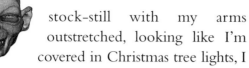

stock-still with my arms outstretched, looking like I'm covered in Christmas tree lights, I was 'captured' by cameras that shoot the dots from 360 degrees. By feeding the information into the computer, I was converted into a virtual Andy Serkis. They turned the monitor around so I could see, and told me to move my arms. Amazingly so did virtual Andy. I carried out some basic movement patterns. They told me that tomorrow we would repeat the process only instead of me on the screen it would be Gollum. I couldn't wait.

The next day, the object of the exercise was to do a workout using the physicality I'd been working on in conjunction with the Gollum model, capturing it for reference for later, creating a catalogue of moves that could be used by the animators to draw from. After that we'd be 'mocapping' part of a scene that might well end up in the final movie.

On went the suit, and away we go, only this time I'd be wearing goggles that would show me in real time what I was doing as Gollum. Ramon explained it was more like controlling or 'driving' a puppet than acting the character, that I had to project life into the Gollum on screen. Thinking I understood what he meant, I donned the goggles. What a buzz! Instantly it made sense. I got into character as Gollum, hunching my back and lowering on to my haunches, splaying my fingers, and in the goggles Gollum responded, simultaneously mirroring my every action, only in a more extreme way. The model already had predetermined muscle and bone structures, which meant I had to do slightly less contortion than, say, if I were playing him in front of a live audience, to achieve the same physical effect.

I was in a totally virtual world of my own. I began to realise the potential for some pretty subtle, understated 'cyber-acting' as I lurked, loped, crawled, shook and slept as Gollum. Eventually, they had to drag me back into the real world, and we prepared to capture the scene where Gollum is leading Frodo and Sam up the treacherously steep steps to Shelob the spider when he catches sight of the Ring on a chain around Frodo's neck and is momentarily consumed with desire for his 'precious'.

Randy and I discussed how we thought the scene ought to be played, and looked at the plate shot with Elijah in it to which we would have to match the action. Then I played the scene, and for the first time I was recorded acting with another performer, even though he wasn't actually there. What came out of the session was that, after playing the scene in a variety of ways, the most truthful version was the stillest and least fussy. Never was there a more bizarre method of learning how to act on screen than this. As Randy pointed out (and this is where his skills as actor-turned-animator really proved their worth), when you're telling a story frame by frame, the temptation is to animate a character to be busy all the time, but it's often more powerful to do nothing. Watching the scene played back is like watching a silent movie where every emotion is carried in 'pantomime'– you really know if you've told the story or not.

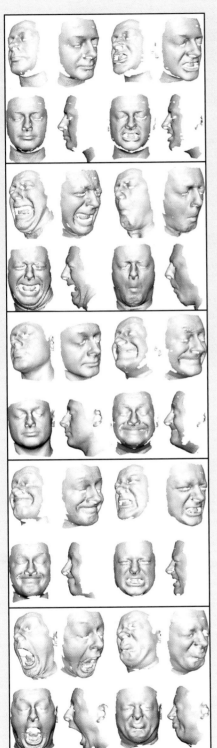

CGI is a useful tool because it's very similar to acting, but you act with 24 frame increments, knowing when to hold a good expression, when to just have a huge reaction, when to have to have him blink (because he's a nervous character and he's got these huge eyes on him), and so on. There are certain things that Gollum has to do which are tricky, because as he's an extreme character, if you're not careful you can get carried away. He's got a little Adam's apple thing in his throat and we once spent way too much time worrying about how often we should see it go up and down when he speaks or reacts. It was easy to get distracted with the small, unimportant stuff because we wanted him to be the best there's ever been. Or going to be – we want Gollum to be other people's benchmark.

The animation is in some ways like traditional cell animation but in three dimensions and actioned on a computer keyboard. You can build in as much movement as you want, so you can animate not only on frames but also between frames, so all the little insects and things moving around faster than 24 times a second can be there too. It's a very versatile process, but ultimately what we try to do is get our character to do something that a living organism could or would do. Most importantly it needs to look like it's 'real' and give a charismatic performance – it's got to have believability, acting craft, and a bit of the magic of cinema!

We did a lot of both photography and scanning of Andy's face in different expressions, but the way a fleshy face moves is very different from the way a fleshless one moves – not so much in the actual mechanics of the musculature, of course, but in the net effect of the bunching of skin and fat and muscle and what those various expressions connote in two different faces. They can express opposite emotions, even though they're doing the same things. A very good maquette was made of Gollum, with features that had echoes of Andy's features, but it was hard to caricature Andy as something thin, so a lot of reference of Andy's exact expressions were taken. The scientific approach would have been to starve Andy and deprive him of sleep for six months, but he wouldn't go for it!

Randall William Cook, Animation Design Supervisor

I spent the following morning having a wander around Wellington when suddenly I got a call from Fran. She told me what scenes were going to be ADR'd and then broke the news that they wanted me to play young Sméagol, which I was delighted about. Young Sméagol is Gollum before he is corrupted by the Ring. He murders his young cousin Déagol so that he can have the Ring for himself. It was going to make so much more sense having the same actor play the part, and it also gave me the chance to actually appear on screen and to play the transformation and decay into Gollum. I went back to the hotel and spent the rest of the day working on the scenes for tomorrow. I met Randy for dinner to discuss the scenes, as he'd been asked to direct the ADR sessions. The great thing was that we were very much on the same wavelength about the character, his addiction to the Ring, and how he responds to situations.

When we came to record ADR the next day, the computer had crashed. Instead I began work with Bay Raitt, who was working on the construction of Gollum's face and how my facial muscles related to his. Bay drew lines all over my face, breaking it up into muscle groups, making a kind of map, after which he scanned my face into the computer. Then he placed me in the centre of a frame with angled mirrors and asked me to perform some basic facial poses, like raising an eyebrow or curling my lips. There was a whole list. By the end I felt as if I'd performed facial gymnastics and had lockjaw!

I really loved working with Bay. We would spend many sessions together over the next couple of years, and I'd always pop by his workstation for a chat and to see how Gollum's face was coming along. He made me laugh because sometimes we'd be in mid-conversation and he'd suddenly say: 'Hey, Andy, sorry, could you just do that again?'

'Do what?'

'You just did this amazing flare with your nostrils.'

'Oh, did I?'

'Yeah, it's incredible, I've never seen anyone who could do that.'

'Well, er... thank you.'

There I was thinking I was saying something interesting and he's looking at my nostril flare.

At the weekend I drove back up to Ohakune where I was going to meet some of the Weta crew to go climbing. We ended up on the western shores of Lake Taupo at Whanganui Bay and had a fantastic day climbing some challenging routes on the rock cliffs nestled into the bay, which was part of a Maori reserve. It was idyllic, and I would recommend anyone to visit this incredibly beautiful region.

Back at the Powderhorn Hotel that evening, I arranged to meet with Keith Stern, whom Ian McKellen had introduced me to. Keith managed Ian's website and we talked about the possibility of creating a site

for me. I had never imagined having one myself but it seemed a valuable tool to connect my past body of work with Gollum: as I would not be appearing 'in the flesh' on screen, I wanted people to realise that I wasn't in fact made of pixels myself. They can now do that at www.serkis.com

I went to bed but couldn't sleep because there was a strange scratching sound in the corner of my room. Then suddenly I woke up… with a mouse sitting on my forehead.

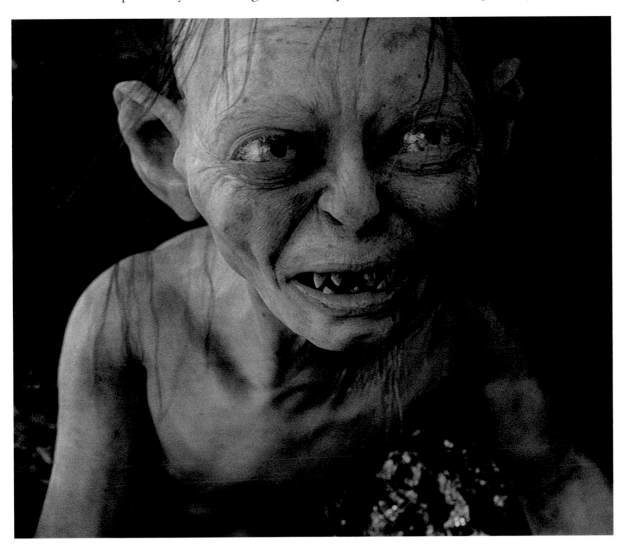

CHAPTER FIVE
Muttering and Gurgling

I just couldn't understand it. I was handed the entire script of films one, two and three and asked to record all of Gollum and Sméagol's dialogue. I felt totally in the dark about the process. Naively, I feared that this would be a definitive voice track from which the animators would work. (It couldn't have been further from the truth: I'm still to record final vocal tracks three years later!) There must have been some miscommunication, but at the time I was devastated. It seemed to defeat the entire object of shooting the scenes with the others if I was going to be recording the voice *before* interacting with Elijah and Sean.

There were no edited scenes on the screen to play off, except the scene in the prologue where Bilbo discovers the Ring and Gollum realises it's gone. I felt in a creative vacuum, which was exactly what I thought we were trying to avoid. But that's what was asked of me so we began our task.

It was here that I first met and worked with Mike Hopkins and Chris Ward, and these would be the first of many, many sessions we'd spend together in the cinema at Camperdown, perfecting Gollum's vocal performance.

Normally, when you are recording dialogue to picture, you stand at a podium with your script, wearing earphones through which you hear back the audio from the filming. Then you watch the screen and synchronise the dialogue to your lips, matching your original performance. In some cases you are required to change the emphasis if the director wants a slightly different reading on a line.

With Gollum, things were different. Firstly, there was no way I could stand up to do the voice – the physical and the vocal were all inextricably linked, and he had to be hunched and on all fours to make the voice work – so Chris had to set the microphone low down to accommodate my physical position. It became a ritual. Secondly, at this stage there was no picture, because we hadn't shot the majority of the scenes, so it was really acting in the dark. Thirdly, I found it very hard to hear myself with earphones on because the way I produce the sound, by constricting my vocal chords, somehow resonates in my ears. If my ears are covered it makes me feel as if I'm semi-deaf!

This was the first real test of vocal stamina. How long could I keep up the voice before my throat would give up? It was quite taxing at first, but like any set of muscles that gets regularly worked on, my vocal chords built up stamina and resistance. We also developed 'Gollum juice' – lemon, honey, ginger and hot water – which I consumed by the bucket-load to keep everything well oiled.

We worked on the Bilbo/Gollum scene. 'When you're ready Andy... take one.'

I launched into it, at a ridiculous pace that was much, much too wildly unfocused and lacked clarity. It was all just bluster and nerves, a blanket of incomprehensible garble. The pressure had got to me, I began to think *I'm never going to be able to sustain this in a million years.*

I tried again, take two. A little slower and more focused but still lacking clarity. Take three, and on we went. I discovered some very interesting things, like it was virtually impossible to say 'l' sounds, as in 'elves'. When we finished the session, I went with Mike to edit the scene together. We used different sections of various takes and constructed a track to be sent to Pete for his approval, even putting a temporary echo effect to simulate Gollum's cave. But I was worried deep down about the prospect of recording the entire role in isolation, especially because I'd spent very little time discussing it with Pete.

After a few days of this I was feeling confused and somewhat deflated. I felt instinctively that this was not the way to go,

so I decided to write a letter to production, explaining how the session had gone and how the work method wasn't quite what I was led to believe it would be. When you're working on a production of this magnitude, you don't really want to add to the pressure everyone's under unless it's very necessary, but this seemed a very important issue to grapple with at this early stage.

That evening I played pool with Dom and Billy at the Hotel Bristol and then we went for a curry. I had one more day of 'experimental' ADR, with Fran and Philippa directing, and then I was supposed to be flying home.

I had a terrible night's sleep obsessing about what the ADR session would hold and whether my letter articulated my concerns accurately enough. The effect of the curry didn't help! Then, to my utter relief, Barrie called me up and completely allayed my fears. The letter was appreciated and taken on board. The purpose of the ADR session had been to give Peter versions of the character to choose between, and also to try and find a clarity within the Gollum delivery. The scene with Bilbo was virtually incomprehensible to a fresh pair of ears and there was concern that New Line would be worried that the American audience would not be able to understand it. Nothing we had recorded so far was definitive, as the scenes being criticised were unedited and not Peter's selected takes anyway. I was so relieved.

Fran, Philippa and I began experimenting with the voice. I tried a range of delivery styles on some pieces of dialogue, which

Capturing and helping to develop the voice for Gollum was a long and interesting journey for the post-production sound team. Mike Hopkins and I began recording with Andy as early as December 1999 to provide some initial test dialogue for the animators to get started with. 'As soon as Andy opened his mouth and we heard what he was capable of we knew that we had truly found our Gollum, and we were pretty sure we wouldn't need to process the voice in any way,' says Mike. 'People find it hard to believe there is no electronic processing applied to the original vocal track to enhance either the texture or timbre of Gollum's voice, and even other sound editors have difficulty believing that the magic is a hundred per cent pure Andy.'

The real challenge was to capture Andy's performance both dynamically and naturally. The aim was to keep all the technology between Andy and the final product as transparent as possible as we didn't want to colour the voice in any way during the recording process. We were very careful with our equipment choices and microphone placement, particularly as we didn't want Andy having to think about anything other than his performance. Although physically very demanding, Andy chose to crouch on all fours when working on the recording stage to ensure his vocal quality was coming from the right part of his body. Many hours were spent in this position, exploring the quality of the voice – initially to ensure that it was intelligible but also to distinguish the finer nuances between the split personalities of Gollum and Sméagol.

In the early days, before the character anmation was fully realised, Andy would perform next to a maquette of Gollum for inspiration, but as the animation development progressed, he could watch himself on a full-sized cinema screen while performing the Gollum voice, seamlessly interacting with the other actors in the scene. This interaction was later tweaked to compliment the rest of the character action by a dedicated team of dialogue editors, Jason Canovas, Ray Beentjes and Martin Kwok, assembling the best of Andy's performances to complete the illusion.

Chris Ward, ADR Recordist

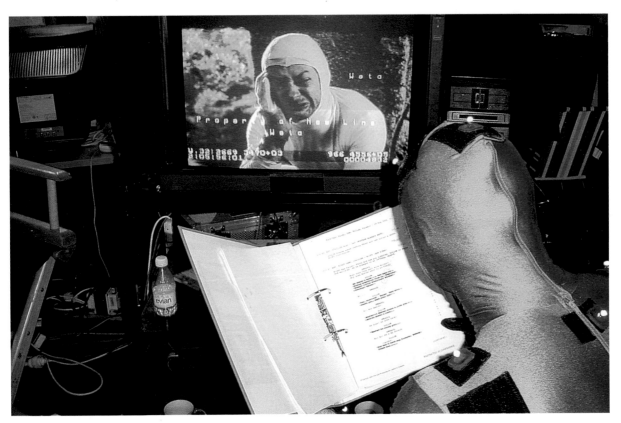

proved to be very illuminating. The slower and more laborious it actually felt, the clearer and more multi-layered the performance.

The general rule of thumb that we arrived at is Sméagol has a higher more nasal tone and speaks more briskly than Gollum, whose tone is lower, slower and more guttural. We also tested out a young Sméagol voice, which is a milder, slightly nasal voice, closer to my own delivery.

Before getting the plane home I was whisked up to the motion capture stage for a last-minute experiment. We were trying to capture movement for Gollum reaching for the Ring as Frodo climbs up the Cirith Ungol stairs, but we were having problems getting the sound to play back in the studio, so that I could synchronise the action. Time was running out and I was beginning to think, *Will I make it home for the birth? I've got to catch this plane.* Eventually Randy Cook had a brainwave. He made a phone call, I think it was to editorial, and they played back the scene from the video deck into the mouthpiece of a phone. Randy held up the handset, and I literally acted out the entire scene, several times, to the faint gurgling tones of Gollum from a good old-fashioned telephone! Low-tech, but effective. As I left for the airport, I thought to myself, *That kind of sums up the way we are making these extraordinary films – a blend of highly sophisticated, ultra-modern technology, and a good deal of boy scout self-reliance.*

On the flight home, I mulled over the

time I had just spent with Gollum, what was good about the process and what was frustrating. I came up with two main positive conclusions:

1– I have to get my head around the fact that this job is going to be fairly gruelling at times, that my journey as an actor on the project is going to be unconventional and unlike anything I've ever done, and the end results are so far away. But the process and discovery each day is the thrill, so I must trust that and take each day at a time.

2– I mustn't get frustrated when at the end of each day we've shot a scene but I never feel like I've completed any-thing. I'm rather envious of Elijah and Sean. At the end of a day's shooting they can take off their Hobbit feet and relax with the firm knowledge that they have completed a scene. It might have gone brilliantly or not as well as they would have liked, but in any event it's 'in the can', done and dusted, and they will never have to do it again. The spontaneity, the mood of the moment, the flicker of genius, or the lack of inspiration, will be there on celluloid, forever. I, on the other hand, feel like I'm in an Escher drawing, with no beginning and no end. I'll never be able to say, 'Well, I certainly nailed that scene!' That won't happen for another two and a half years. Be patient Serkis.

And then all of a sudden these demons came out to play:

3– Be prepared Serkis. Be prepared for the worst. Remember, at the end of it, there is no guarantee that it will succeed. In fact Gollum could be disastrous and millions of Tolkien fans will declare a 'Fatwah' on your head and you'll have to change your identity and be forced to live on an island somewhere. Years of your life will have been wasted, your children will grow up to hate you because you were never there in their early years. They won't even walk down the street with you because their school friends will snigger and point at 'the man who wore spandex'. You'll never work again, your credibility will be shot to pieces, you'll go down in history as the man who spoilt a masterpiece. Leave now while there's still time. Go on Serkis, pay someone to break your legs, there's still time, no one will even notice you've left!

I realised I now had Gollum under my skin, and he would be there for quite some time, warts and all. Which was now quite a worrying thought as I was heading home to my loved ones.

As the car pulled up outside our house, I saw the sign. 'WELCOME HOME DADDY' painted in bright colours. I looked around, there were leaves on the trees, it was summer. The front door opened and there they were. I scooped up Ruby (who had grown inches

taller) in my arms, and held Lorraine, who was so very close to the big day.

Sonny was born on 6 June 2000 in a birthing pool in our living room. It was a gloriously sunny day, I could go on forever about it. Sonny was this tiny thing who looked *exactly* like me. He was all wet from the pool and had that innocent but wise look that babies have, as if they've seen it all before. An amazing squashed-up, old-man face on top of a pristine white baby body. He really reminded me of Sméagol. It sounds awful – my son's just been born and I'm associating him with a wretched Ring junkie. But I mention it because Sonny and Ruby were both to influence many decisions about how Sméagol became defined in my head. The unfathomable contradiction between the innocence of childhood and the loss of that innocence were themes that we'd explore. Fran was also working with these ideas, and drew a lot from her own children as she was writing.

Time shot by and we barely had time to draw breath, apart from a wonderful holiday for a week in Devon, before we were making plans to return to New Zealand, this time as a family.

Jet lag on your own is pretty testing, but when there are four people's body clocks going haywire, it really can be disorientating. We were staying at the Duxton Hotel until we could get a house sorted out, and Ruby would ask to go to the park at two o'clock in the morning. We spent quite a few nights running up and down the corridors until we could get an early breakfast. We even played on the big slides by the waterfront in the moonlight. Everything but sleep. Sonny had developed an unbelievable cough – it sounded as if his ribs were going to break – and we wondered if bringing them over had been such a good idea.

On my first day back at work, I had to go to the Weta Workshop to have a full head cast made. This was to enable the special effects make-up team to make the prosthetics for the transformation from young Sméagol to Gollum. This was when I first got to know the immensely talented senior prosthetics advisor Gino Acevedo. My face was covered in Vaseline and then painted with alginate (a warm gooey paste which hardens), then covered with plaster of Paris. It took time to

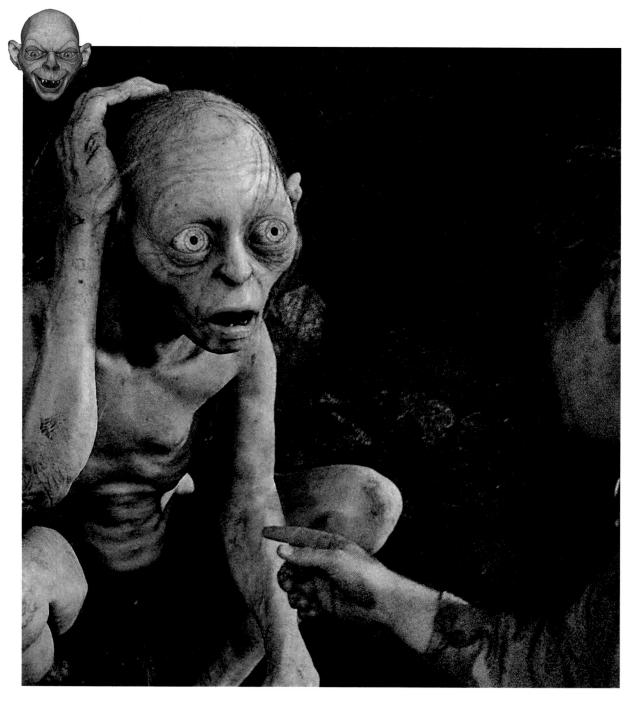

do and I was warned that some actors can feel claustrophobic and was told to signal if there was a problem.

My whole head was encased down to my shoulders. Every now and then someone would say, 'Are you OK Andy?' and I'd give them a thumbs up. But I was so tired I got drowsy and after about twenty minutes I fell into a deep sleep. Apparently, I just stopped responding, and they were beginning to wonder if I'd be the first case of murder by plaster of Paris.

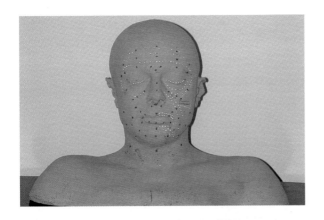

We finally moved into our house in Miramar in September 2000. It was close enough to walk to work, which was great. The weekend before I started filming, we took a trip to a wild seal colony at Cape Palliser, a two and a half hour drive away from Wellington. It was pretty remote and incredibly windy and Ruby could hardly stand up, but we found the seals. You have to remember not to get between them and the sea or else they feel threatened, which is fine in theory, but they're pretty well camouflaged. So, of course, we found ourselves with the sea behind us and some very unhappy, barking hulks lolloping towards us. At that moment my brand-new Weta baseball cap blew off my head and landed right near the gaping jaws of the mother of all seals. For a second I

thought of getting it back, then sense prevailed and we ran.

On the way back it started to rain, horizontally, and so hard that the wipers couldn't keep up, and then we saw the strangest sight. From nowhere, a woman in her seventies was walking in the middle of the road towards our car. It was almost impossible to make her out with all the rain and I could easily have run her over. We pulled up and she explained that she'd fallen asleep at the wheel of her car and driven off the road, down a steep ravine and into a river. Miraculously all she'd done was chip a tooth. We started to drive her back to her village, which was quite a few miles away, and she phoned her husband to come and meet us along the way. She was in shock, but holding it together. At last we saw the headlights of her husband's car, and as we both pulled up, he wound down his window, lent out and caustically remarked to her, 'So you missed the bridge? Oh well, shit happens.'

Lorraine and I were flabbergasted at the seemingly dispassionate response to his elderly wife's near-fatal experience. But of course these people are tough Kiwis who aren't easily shaken. You just don't make a fuss. When I went down the bottom of the ravine with him to inspect the car – it was practically written off – he merely said, 'You woulda thought she coulda driven it back up the other side.' He casually leant in through the broken windows and, no joke, pulled out a six-pack of beer, then just strolled back to his car. I thought to myself, *That's why* The Lord of the Rings *is being made here, because the people are made of steel.*

CHAPTER SIX
The Taming of Sméagol

The introduction of Gollum really takes place at Emyn Muil, as he climbs down the cliff and gets close to his 'precious' before Frodo and Sam launch an attack, surprising him. A vicious fight breaks out with Gollum scrabbling to get the Ring, biting Sam, and ending up with Frodo producing Sting and holding it to Gollum's throat. I was interested in finding a way to play the transition from the aggressive Gollum to the moment he gives in – which Tolkien beautifully describes as 'Gollum collapsed and went as loose as wet string' – because it needed to completely defy the audience's expectation of who they thought this vicious little creature was.

A fight had been choreographed by Steve Reinsfield and Tim Wong, the stunt men (or 'stunties' as they were affectionately called), which Elijah, Sean and I then modified to make it our own, before showing it to Pete who then blocked it out with his ideas. One thing he was very keen to pursue was to end the fight in a tableau that completely replicated the amazing Alan Lee illustration that features in *The Lord of the Rings* centenary edition. This has Gollum on his back with his legs wrapped

around Sam, and Frodo pulling Gollum's head back by his hair with Sting at his throat. We shuffled into those positions, and then worked backwards to see how the fight could lead us into them. Then we put in some moves that worked with the geography of the rocky set, like Gollum crawling up the rock before jumping on to Frodo. Finally we slowly blocked the set piece out for camera.

For the master shot, a motion-controlled camera was used so that after we'd shot it with me on camera, the shot could be replicated exactly with just Elijah and Sean miming where I was, and then a plate shot with no actors in, just for the background.

We then rehearsed again and again, starting slowly at first and building up speed. I had been psyching myself up for this scene for ages. We were all ready, and at last Pete shouted 'action' and the three of us went at it hell for leather. At the end all three of us fell to the floor, exhausted. Sean had lost a Hobbit toe and my lungs were on fire. We waited for words from Pete only to hear, 'Er, yeah, yeah that was OK, it just needs a bit

more energy, guys.' We spent a whole day shooting the fight sequence, and must have done it thirty times.

The following scene was Gollum being dragged by a rope by Sam, and swearing on the 'precious' to serve the master of the Ring, Frodo. Gollum promises to lead them to the Black Gates of Mordor. My instincts on this scene were to play Gollum as a manipulative child throwing a tantrum to get his own way, and then playing the sympathy inducing passive-aggressive child as he swears on the Ring and Frodo releases him from the rope. In this way Gollum's melodramatic theatrics would allow some humour, which is also a vital part of the character. We laugh at him because he's so pathetic. I based this very much on experiences of trying to pull Ruby out of a supermarket when she was trying to hang on to the shelves full of sweets. She would throw herself to the ground and writhe around as if the world was coming to an end, and shoppers all around would stop and look in horror. I'd often found myself in Sam's shoes when he says, 'Every Orc in Mordor's gonna hear this racket!' This scene, like many we shot during principal photo-graphy, would develop in the future to incorporate other, deeper levels when we reworked it on the motion capture stage a year and a half later, but this was my initial take on it.

A considerable amount of the Emyn Muil sequence was directed by veteran director Geoff Murphy. He had made, among others, cult Kiwi films such as *Utu* and *Goodbye Porkpie* in the 1970s and was now lending his vast experience to this epic. He's definitely a man who knows what he's about and cuts a very distinctive figure with his tall, Lee Marvinesque appearance, dressed in a long battered leather coat and permanently hunched over a cigarette. On the first day we worked together, he eyed me suspiciously as I walked on to set, giving me the 'What the

hell is this one wearing?' look that I'd come to recognise. After the first take, I heard his rasping voice from behind the monitor and was wondering what he was going to make of this. All of a sudden, he stood up and plainly announced, 'Jesus, I didn't think overacting was possible on this picture 'til I saw you.'

The legend goes that in four years of filming we all had such a great time and no one ever got miffed about anything, but around this time there was a short spell when things got very dark for me and Gollum's vitriol began to flow into Andy's veins. Boy, am I glad that this wasn't featured on any of the DVDs! The art of cyber-thespianism completely lost its charms for me on one particular day…

I hate what I'm doing, I hate the fact that I only get one or two chances to get my performance, and even then it doesn't seem to make any difference 'cause nobody seems to have a clue what I'm doing. Why am I here? I know Gollum's going to be animated but I've still got to be able to give my performance. I hate the fact my shots are called 'reference passes' and then when I step off camera and it's just on Elijah and Sean it's 'OK, now we're gonna do it for real.' So, what, my shots aren't for real? I'm busting a gut here, for what? I wish I was doing this in prosthetics, I'm sure everybody would take this more seriously. I've got months and months of this, I've really had it, I can't do it anymore. I wish I was doing a normal character, I mean at least the other guys have got costumes and make-up to help them into the world of their characters, what have I got? A poxy stretchy rotten suit which I HATE.'

I've cleaned up the language for family reading, but as you can see I was definitely not a happy ex-Hobbit. And on this day, Sean, Elijah and I had a little bit of a set to. We've talked about it since and worked out what it was. They had been working very hard on *The Fellowship of the Ring* and were psychologically at a place of 'We're only a third of the way there.' I, on the other hand, was full of Gollum and wanted to let it out. I was wired to the max.

Our working process was still in its infancy, and there were grey areas. There seemed to be this sense of shooting it, with me on camera, as some kind of 'warm up' to the real event, which was when Sean and Elijah would then act the scene with me off camera. From their point of view, they knew I was there to act the scene with them, but in the back of their minds I was always going to be replaced, so instead of acting with me in the moment, they were practising for the 'real' take. On one of my shots they'd lost concentration and were giggling, so I had a go at them, trying to explain that I was only getting one take to define my performance. They both apologised, and so did I, the air cleared and it was a bit of a turning point, because actually it opened up a great discussion about how this whole process works and where it was not working. Ironically, in the final version in *The Two Towers*, a lot of the shots where we are physically connected, like the fight sequence, Peter chose to use the 'reference' passes and have the animators paint frame by frame over my performance, because the energy in the scene worked better between the three of us. That became the key – reciprocal energy. It

was becoming apparent that, from an acting perspective, this CG character would only work if the energy between us was real.

Life at Townsend Road, Miramar, was settling into a routine. Lorraine had begun to make a network of friends with parents of children who were going to nursery at Miramar community centre, which Ruby was attending. Sonny was having a tough start to his life with the cough from hell.

One day, we took the cable car fromLampton Quay up to the botanical gardens that overlook the entire harbour. It's a heavenly place. But it was in this 'garden of Eden' that Ruby, not even two years old, first displayed a shocking abuse of power over her baby brother. From out of the blue, she bit his tiny finger so hard that her teeth marks remained embedded in his flesh for ages. Sonny screamed his lungs out. We were speechless. What had made her do it? I quickly talked to her about what a nasty thing that was to do, she got upset and then we all made friends.

About half an hour later she did it again. This time I pulled her away and told her off more firmly. An hour later she bit him again.

That evening, as we sat around the dinner table in silence, I looked at my daughter with fresh eyes. It was as if she had lost some of her innocence. She had discovered a new power and was learning how to wield it. She was looking at me as if to say, 'So, what are you going to do about it?' Lorraine and I thought that she might be jealous because her baby brother was getting a lot of attention, but it was the repetition of the action that had really shocked me, the conscious decision to do it again. That enjoyment of power began to play on my mind. The possibility of being cruel and enjoying the pain you're causing others, at such a young age. Maybe it was a gut survival response to feeling usurped.

As I was trying to analyse my daughter's behaviour, my mind flipped over to Sméagol. Was he born malicious? Did he grow up with a nasty streak in him? Gandalf implies that he was weak and easily susceptible to the Ring's power. Frodo is stronger and doesn't fall prey to the Ring as easily. Would Frodo have maliciously bitten a baby's finger as a child? Probably not. Would Sméagol have? I think so. I remembered my own childhood, spending summer holidays in the Middle East, knocking the tails off tiny lizards with swipe from a bamboo stick. I can't believe I used to do that. Maybe it was a bizarre kind of curiosity, a fascination, an experiment with power. One thing was for certain – Sméagol was definitely 'curious minded'.

Ithilien was calling, and for that we had to fly south to Queenstown, adventure sports capital of the world. Encircled by stunning mountain ranges, including 'The Remarkables', Queenstown is a cool town of hip bars and restaurants sitting alongside the shore of the vast lake Wakatipu. The scenery is breathtaking. A magnificent place to be on location filming.

Unfortunately Sonny's cough got worse and worse, to the point where we had to take him to the local hospital. We were told that he had the symptoms of croup, a vicious chest infection that can affect small children. We were very worried. I'd never heard anyone

cough like this. The sound was unearthly, and so loud for such a tiny little frame.

We were staying at Spinnaker Bay, some self-catering apartments right by the water's edge, where Sean and Elijah were also staying. From there we'd have a thirty-minute drive south to Twelve Mile Delta, where we'd be filming the Ithilien scenes, the first of these being the 'rabbit scene'.

This, for me, was a particular favourite in the script as it was then, because it was one of the first scenes we'd shot that dwelled on characters and the developing relationship between Frodo, Sam and Gollum. Sam is beginning to feel usurped by Gollum, there is a rift growing between Frodo and Sam, and now Gollum is invading Sam's culinary territory by catching food for his master. There was a real feeling of sibling rivalry between them. As we began to shoot the scene, it felt like we had all hit our stride together as a team of actors and crew. It's hard to explain, but the process seemed to invade less and less, and we really began to play off each other.

Gollum gallops in and excitedly drops two dead rabbits on to Frodo's lap, impressing on him that, 'they are young and tender' and that he must, 'eat them, eat them'. He then starts gobbling them up, but Sam quickly intervenes and protests, 'there's only one way to eat a brace of coneys' – cut to Sam cooking them in a pot. Gollum goes nuts and they start to argue about their favourite food. Meanwhile Frodo hears something in the bushes and sneaks off.

I had two real dead rabbits, one of which had been given some rather gruesomely

realistic innards that I could pull out of its stomach with my teeth. I felt that Gollum should move like an over-excited puppy bringing his master his slippers in a very over familiar and ingratiating way. Also he is genuinely hungry and is delighted with himself for catching his prey, prompting a

victorious dance of triumph with a quick, defiant shake of the fist to the 'Yellow Face' sun, his old enemy.

We shot the opening wide shot, again using a motion-controlled camera, so that the shot could be repeated in the manner I've described before, and then we shot the close-ups. I was really starting to enjoy playing Gollum at last, and Sean and I really enjoyed

playing the growing antagonism between Sam and Gollum, especially because the debate was over the relatively mundane subject of food. As an actor it's so important to feel freed up and relaxed so that you can really play the moment and let the character take you places you hadn't necessarily planned. They are always the most joyous moments, when you completely take yourself by surprise. When this starts happening on

a regular basis, it means you are flowing with the character, and this was the day it began for me.

11 October 2000 was a very special birthday, exactly one year since *The Lord of the Rings* started principal photography. To celebrate, production organised a huge lunch on set, with a band and, of course, a cake. It was a great occasion, and aptly marked the journey, joining other milestones such as '1000th slate', '133 days of shooting – halfway there!', and the countless other crew and cast birthdays that were celebrated along the way. Not least of those was Ruby's, whose second birthday was a few days later, and we had a great party for her and all the *Rings* children who were staying in Queenstown.

The rocky Cirith Ungol set had remained inside the school gymnasium for over a year, patiently waiting for everyone to return and complete the scene. It had been started in the early months of principal photography, before I'd been scheduled to start. The weather had turned bad, and so that they could continue shooting, they had opted to shoot a sequence of the scene in which Gollum accuses Sam of eating the Lembas bread and convinces Frodo that Sam is lying. Sam attacks Gollum but Frodo intervenes, siding with Gollum, and tells Sam that he can come no further with them.

As I hadn't arrived at that point, Randy had stood in for Gollum and Andrew Jack, the dialect coach, performed the dialogue. It was very strange watching footage of a scene that I'd not been party to, and then having to join in, literally falling into shot after Sam attacks Gollum. When the raw footage was eventually cut together, it was hilarious. You see Sean striking Randy who falls out of frame, and then Andy falls into the next frame and the fight continues. We eventually got to reshoot the scene on the motion capture stage, two years later, so this scene must probably take the prize for 'most protracted process'.

At the same location, at the bottom of the Cirith Ungol set, a section of rocky scree had been built to represent the foot of the rocky bluff overlooking the Black Gates of Mordor. Sam had fallen and Frodo had slid after him and hidden him under his cloak from the Easterling soldiers. We were going to shoot what happened next. Frodo and Sam are about to make a dash before the gates shut when suddenly Gollum lunges forward and hauls them back, wildly protesting to Frodo that they will be caught and that they mustn't let the 'precious' find its way back to 'Him'. He promises to lead them via another way into Mordor.

'And action!'

I leapt through the air, grabbing Sean and Elijah's cloaks, accidentally catching hold of Sean's wig in the process. As I yanked them both backwards Sean's wig literally took off, and was suddenly airborne, landing a great distance away. Elijah and I collapsed in a helpless heap, as did Pete who called cut. It was quite shocking. In all the months of

shooting, a wig had never come off and then suddenly, in a flash, the desperate reality of Frodo's quest turned into this surreal comedy!

We watched it back on the monitor. It looked as if I'd ripped Sam's head off! Sean wasn't amused in the slightest – I knew it must've hurt him, because those wigs are pretty much bolted to your head, so having it ripped off would really be painful, but at the time he was so angry and I didn't know why. So I got angry back. It felt like we were going

to come to blows. I imagined the headlines in the local press – 'GOLLUM AND SAM IN WIG WHAM!' The rest of the scene had an extra level of reality to the antagonism between Sam and Gollum.

During time off we got to see some pretty spectacular scenery. We visited the pristine forests near Glenorchy, which were used in the films to represent Lothlórien. We flew over the breathtaking mountains, waterfalls and hanging valleys into Fiordland National Park, and cruised down Milford Sound to the famous Mitre Peak. In Queenstown itself we

often took the skyline gondola up the mountain, which gives stunning panoramic views over the whole area, and where we spent hours getting our adrenalin fix on the luge track. One of our favourite haunts was the Queen's Pavilion, a hexagonal Edwardian bathing house, now café, right on the lakeside, where we'd relax and eat, while Ruby spent a lot of time playing on the slide and swings of the adventure playground built thoughtfully next to it. I'm beginning to sound like a travel guide so I'll stop. Actually, if you do want a great guidebook, check out Ian Brodie's New Zealand bestseller, *The Lord of the Rings Location Guidebook*.

Ian, you owe me a pint.

CHAPTER SEVEN

'Give us that, Déagol, my love'

When we got back to Wellington, I had to go straight to wardrobe for a costume fitting with Ngila Dickson, for the young Sméagol scenes in which I'd actually appear in the flesh. I was so in awe of the work she had done and was very excited about the prospect of working with her. I was also thrilled because I was going to wear a real costume. After months and months in the gimp suit, trousers were going to be a real pleasure!

Ngila had designed a costume and then worked with me, taking on board some of the character ideas I'd been thinking about. She had come up with the idea of tying Sméagol's clothes into the fishing culture of the Stoor Hobbits, as they were water folk, who lived and worked the River Anduin and the Gladden Fields. An oiled canvas smock and heavy-duty tweed trousers were brought out and tried on. A rope belt was added and it began to feel like it was coming together.

We did some work on Gollum – although he's now a CG creation that Weta made, they thought originally he may be a mixture of person and puppet, and so we did design a bit of a rag to put round his genitalia. Then, when Andy arrived – and he's just the most wonderful person on the planet – Peter and Fran and everyone else immediately saw that he was so right for the part and so full of ideas that they rethought things. Indeed, it was because of Andy that they put in that sequence of how Sméagol becomes Gollum by murdering Déagol and then disappears off into the mountains. So we had to do what we call a 'breakdown', where you take clothing and slowly destroy it for each successive shot. Everyone loves a good bit of breakdown. Andy was so into it he would come in and show me all the positions he would go through, and we would slash and burn the costume a bit more according to his posture.

Ngila Dickson, Costume Designer

I was interested in trying to define Gollum's class and status in the community, and had thought that, coming from the wealthiest and largest Stoor family, he would probably never have really worked a day in his life. He probably skipped school and spent time squandering money that he had stolen from his grandmother's purse. It was a matriarchy and his grandmother was the head of his family, so I wondered how we might reflect this. We decided that some sort of neckerchief, maybe made of silk and a little flamboyant, might be a good idea. I liked the idea of carrying through the drug addict metaphor, implying that he was like a young rich kid who had always had money in his pocket and was able to experiment with whatever took his fancy, like a Middle-earth version of a young playboy or a Victorian dandy.

We also examined the idea of his curious and inquisitive nature. I always saw Sméagol as a loner, not particularly liked, a bit of a Billy-no-mates, and not very good at team sports. He would have been thought of as a bit weird and he would have secretly dreamed up revengeful scenarios for all the other Stoor Hobbits who completely ignored him. So, to cope with being so introverted and alienated, he became a collector, obsessed with the 'roots and beginnings' of things. Objects became more important than people, at least they couldn't hurt him. Physically, I gave him a stoop from constantly looking down. I imagined him to be fairly narcissistic, spending hours fascinating himself by staring at his own reflection in the water while he fished. We decided to display this obsessive

behaviour through shiny pau shell buttons, and little trophies of fish bones tied to his belt, as if he were adorning himself with fetish-like status symbols. Although he was dysfunctional, he was not evil or malicious, just, as the Travis Bickle character says of himself in *Taxi Driver*, full of 'morbid self-attention'.

Once we had established the costume we then had to take it through all the stages of decomposition as Sméagol becomes corrupted by the Ring and descends into madness, becoming Gollum. These clothes would eventually become a ragged loincloth that hangs by a thread on Gollum's emaciated body. We had a further two identical costumes which we 'broke down', Ngila hacking away at the cloth while it was hanging on me so we could create the progressive stages of wear and tear.

The next stop was a hair and make-up test. Peter King had created a wig for Sméagol, which again would have to match the eventual hairline of the balding Gollum. In order to make the wig work with my face shape, we needed to raise my hairline to make the forehead more prominent, so out came the razor and within minutes I looked like I'd had a frontal lobotomy. Once the wig was on it really began to make sense, and

then Peter applied a pallid skin tone to wash out my skin colour, as if Sméagol constantly kept out of the sun.

Then Gino arrived with the ears. He applied them and then layered subtle shades of make-up with his airbrush to blend the edges so that they were invisible.

And there we were. This was the first stage of Sméagol's journey into hell. Gino took photos and some video footage so that Peter could approve the look. While this was all going on I finally met Thomas Robbins, who was going to play Déagol.

Thomas had worked with Peter and Fran on *Forgotten Silver*, the brilliant 1995 mockumentary about a fictitous Kiwi who invented filmmaking. We were both really looking forward to shooting the scene together. And a few days later we'd all moved over the Rimutaka Ranges into the Wairarapa and were ready to shoot.

John Mahaffie, second unit director, who'd spent months shooting a great deal of the Helm's Deep sequence, was to direct the scene with Fran and Philippa. As we all arrived at the lodge at Fernside, I began to get psyched up to play the key moment when the Ring 'found' Sméagol. That night I couldn't sleep at all. The hours went by slowly and then, just as I started to doze, the alarm went off.

We got into costume, but it had started to drizzle by the time we came out of the make-up truck. We went down on to the location, which was absolutely perfect. It really matched Tolkien's description, an idyllic lake with great beds of flowers and reeds. But the rain was getting heavier and John and Fran had really wanted it to be sunny, to accentuate the sense of it being like the Garden of Eden, so that when the 'sin' is committed the mood breaks as darkness falls. It couldn't have been more gloomy, and eventually it was decided to abandon the day and wait until tomorrow, when the weather was forecast to be clear. That afternoon, however, the rain stopped and we managed to rehearse, so that we could launch straight into it, first thing.

The next day was glorious, and before we knew it Thomas and I, Déagol and Sméagol, were sitting in our coracle, fishing in the middle of the lake. In the scene, Déagol catches a fish, but can't reel it in – it's too powerful and ends up pulling him into the water. I decided to play the scene with Sméagol enjoying seeing his cousin panic when suddenly Déagol disappears and he begins to panic himself, as I imagined him rather prone to outbursts of *schadenfreude*. I suffer from it myself. It's a horrible trait, and because I know it's going to happen I can usually control it, but in the most dire scenarios which demand sympathy or sadness, I'm still capable of nervously reacting with a giggle. I expect I'll have to see a shrink about it one day.

We shot a close-up of Sméagol skewering a worm with a fishing hook, which would be inserted into the boat sequence. (Sean Foot drew a brilliant picture of it in his notebook that day and gave it to me.) We tried it a few different ways, with varying degrees of sadistic enjoyment of the pain he was causing the worm, and that pure childlike fascination at the behaviour of the worm as it was being hooked (rather like Ruby biting Sonny). Basically we were looking for the right level to introduce the character's moral stature. By the way, no worms were harmed in the making of this motion picture (and their agents had negotiated them great rates for additional stunt work).

Finally, we came to the moment where Déagol climbs out of the water, clasping something in his hand. Sméagol appears, relieved that his cousin has not drowned, and then sees the Ring for the first time, glistening in Déagol's palm. The million-dollar question was how quickly should he fall prey to its power? The first time we played it, I let the Ring overwhelm him in a flash, so that he grabbed Déagol by the throat and, like a disassociated psychotic, went through the whole murder without looking at him once, completely emotionally detached. It felt right, but John and Fran were keen to pursue other routes so that we'd have choices later. I was going to be working alongside Fran with her directing in the future and already thought she was a wonderfully challenging and accurate director. I admired her approach, which enabled so many varied choices.

We tried versions of varying degrees, where he was more connected to the act he was committing but powerless to stop himself, where he became almost erotically charged by the Ring's power, and where he was almost weeping as he kills Déagol. We played the scene many times – Tom's neck was red raw by the end of it.

The scene ends with Sméagol taking the Ring from Déagol's dead hand and putting it on. Again the choices were infinite. Is he racked with guilt? Does he feel any remorse at all? Is he too driven by lust to care? And then, as if on cue, during the last few takes, ominous clouds rolled in, turning the sunlit idyll into a dark, foreboding place.

Back to Wellington and shooting the transformation scene. Some beautifully detailed small sets had been constructed in which we could play out the gradual fall of Sméagol and the emergence of Gollum. The day before we were to shoot, Fran and I talked about how the corruption should manifest itself, using the different environments and progressively deteriorating make-up. I was also keen that we'd see a physical journey

The Sméagol to Gollum sequence wasn't in our original screenplay; it was something that we decided to do while we were shooting. Fran directed it, because as it wasn't in our schedule there was no available time for me to shoot it.

Fran and Andy really worked very closely together to shoot this little sequence that showed him becoming Gollum. We wanted to make it very clear that Gollum wasn't always the way he is, and this is what happens to you if the Ring ends up overpowering you and you're unable to give it up. We felt that showing the transformation was ultimately going to be the most potent way of selling the idea to the audience.

Peter Jackson, Director

from upright Sméagol to crawling Gollum. So we constructed several vignettes that showed his growing loneliness, paranoia, addiction to the Ring and his self-imposed exile from the world.

That night I shaved my chest, arms, legs, the lot. The next morning I had an early make-up call with Gino, around 3.30 a.m. The first stage was Sméagol being shunned by his family and running into the wilderness. He is full of self-pity and he rails at the injustice of being told to leave. At this stage the make-up was similar to the Déagol scene, but as the day progressed I'd have several big changes.

The next phase was seeing him literally getting his fix from the Ring's exquisite power. Here we see the agony and the ecstasy as he draws it in. He begins to convulse, and the involuntary 'Gollum, Gollum' gurgles in his throat for the first time. This sound, the defining moment where he really begins to lose the Sméagol part of his personality, felt like it was a muscle spasm, almost like a Tourette's syndrome sufferer, the association of guilt locked into his mind at the moment of the murder. We started to introduce the prosthetic make-up with the change in his teeth, which were evolving into decaying, but sharper, animal molars. It was such a joy from an acting point of view to be able to chart this part of the character's journey, and with Fran's inspiring direction, it was a really fascinating and enjoyable time.

Now it was time for the first big make-up change. The accelerated ageing process was kicking in (I know all about this – mine kicked in years ago!) Gino and his team worked fast like a pit stop crew, attaching a bald cap with layers of thinning hair. A latex half-mask was applied, and meticulously airbrushed with veins and broken skin, and then my entire body was airbrushed with a putrid greenish wash, then highlighted with scars, cuts and other abrasions. Semi-opaque contact lenses were fitted. Gino manicured my nails with a small drilling tool to give them that stumpy gnarled jagged feel.

We jumped him forward to a time when he'd been totally isolated for years. He'd started to get paranoid, spending a lot of time on his haunches waiting over pools for fish to pass by, which he'd catch with his bare hands and gorge on their raw flesh. He'd started to talk to himself, repeating his defence of why

We did four different stages of transformation make-up on Andy.

*Stage One: Make-up artist Peter Owen and me turned Andy into 'basic' Sméagol.
Peter shaved Andy's front hairline back about two inches, which allowed us to apply a wig
and give Sméagol a very high forehead, and I applied gelatin Hobbit ears over Andy's ears. We
designed Sméagol's and Déagol's ears to look a bit different to those on Frodo and the others
because these two Hobbits were a 'river folk' type. The prosthetic ears were designed by Jamie
Beswarick, one of Weta's very talented sculptors, and the edges of the ears were very thin so they
blended right into the natural contours of Andy's ears. They were then coloured to match Andy's
skin tone.*

*Stage Two: The Ring has begun to take him over, which causes him to look very sickly and
diseased. To illustrate that, Sméagol has begun to lose a few teeth, so we made Andy some dentures
to cover his own teeth, giving the illusion that they are becoming very rotten. Peter Owen then
changed the colour of his skin by applying a very pale tone and adding some purples and blues
under his eyes, again to make him look very sickly. I airbrushed some very fine and subtle veins
on his skin to make it look as though it was becoming very thin and transparent. About a month
prior to this, I had asked Andy not to cut his fingernails so that on the day I could really roughen
up the edges.*

*Stage Three: When Sméagol runs away to the hills and hides, we really had to change his
appearance, which required a special gelatin facial appliance that was sculpted by John Craney,
another of Weta's sculptors. This had a smaller nose and higher cheekbones – some of the features
that would also be in the final CG Gollum. We added a bald cap, which I then coloured with a
lot of veins and age spots. These blended in really well with a new wig, which was very thin and
sparse to give the impression that he was beginning to really lose his hair. We used different
dentures with even fewer teeth and more decay. Finally, wanting to change the look of Andy's eyes,
we had him wear some very pale, light blue contact lenses.*

*Stage Four: For the final transformation, we made a full silicone head, face and finger extensions
for Andy, which brought Gollum even closer to the CG version. This was applied by make-up
artists Bill Hunt, Ben Hawker, Sean Foot, Rogier Samuels and me. Besides this additional make-
up to Andy's head, we also applied a 'hump' to his back before painting his whole body a very
sickly pale colour. This stage of make-up took five hours to apply.*

*The final stage was when the CG character came to life thanks to Weta Digital. The model that
the digital artists worked from was sculpted by Jamie Beswarick and Ben Wootten of Weta and I
was very fortunate to be asked to help capture Gollum's skin tones on the computer alongside
texture painter Sergei Nevshupov.*

Andy was a complete trooper throughout these make-up tortures – indeed he loved it all!

Gino Acevedo, *Senior Prosthetics Supervisor*

he'd killed Déagol. Time and the elements, plus the addiction to the 'precious' was taking its toll. He was insane, driven, full of self-loathing and hatred for the world. We shot a sequence of him sitting crouched on a rock, and slowly and unemotionally pulling out clumps of his own hair. It was as if he knew he was suffering the effects of a horrible terminal disease.

The final stage of his transformation required a long make-up change. A full head and shoulders latex mask was applied and a misshapen spine piece was glued to my back. Finger extensions, decomposed teeth and totally opaque lenses which were almost impossible to see out of, worked well for shutting me off inside my own head. The costume was now dirty rags hanging off my body. I was almost totally unrecognisable. There wasn't a single inch of my body that wasn't covered in make-up. Lorraine brought the children in to visit me. I was slightly concerned that they would be freaked out, but Ruby immediately spotted it was me underneath the elaborate disguise, and after looking me up and down,

64

she shook her head and said 'Silly Daddy' rather dismissively.

The last part of the journey before he becomes CG Gollum (which I had now began to justify in my own head as an advanced state of possession by the Ring) was seeing him leave the sun, the 'Yellow Face', that watched him and burnt him, as he metaphorically leaves the world behind and crawls into the dark dank caves inside the Misty Mountains. He is now on all fours, his taut ageing skin tears as he rubs against rocks. We see him take one last look around before worming his way into the cold darkness of his tomblike cell, where he can be alone with his 'precious'. The last moment we played was him full of craven lust as he clasps the Ring close, thinking he'll have it forever.

We had to make everyone in the audience understand who Gollum and Sméagol were. We decided quite early on that he had to be very important to Frodo as well, because of his own destiny – as Galadriel showed him, he could go the same way. Andy got that very quickly and developed the stages of deterioration, just giving us so many levels, so many wonderful things, and we feel like that's the reason the audience is going to be interested in this creature – they have been given a very real performance which cements the relationship between him and Frodo. So his deterioration scenes became even more important.

Philippa Boyens, Co-writer

CHAPTER EIGHT
Morgul Vale

One of the greatest thrills for me during principal photography was meeting Sir Edmund Hillary, the famous Kiwi mountaineer who, along with Tensing Norgay, first climbed to the summit of Everest in 1953. As a passionate climber myself, there is really no greater living hero I could possibly wish to meet. We were shooting a sequence for *The Return of the King* where Frodo, Sam and Gollum pass the decapitated statue of the Gondorian king in the valley of Morgul, actually north-west of Wellington in Waitarere Forest.

I'll never forget Peter saying that Hillary was coming down to visit the set. I don't really get star-struck but this man had been such a boyhood hero of mine I must admit I was quite nervous. Peter had told us stories about how Hillary, who had an irrepressible energy, would get up in the middle of the night and, without oxygen, cut steps in the ice up to a new camp. Like the fairytale of the elves and the shoemaker, the other British climbers would wake up to find all this work had been done.

A table was set up in the woods, and this rather extraordinary lunch party took place. I eventually found a moment to ask Sir Edmund about climbing Mount Cook (New Zealand's highest mountain) as I had a growing desire to attempt it at some point. Peter had arranged very generously for copies of Sir Edmund's autobiography to be brought down for Sean, Elijah and me, and he signed mine, '*To Gollum, best wishes, Ed Hillary*.' Awesome.

A couple of days later, we returned to that location to shoot the final scene in *The Two Towers*. Gollum convinces Sméagol in a schizophrenic monologue that they should lead the Hobbits to 'her', the evil Shelob. Peter was intent on shooting this scene in one long continuous take, and so he and I rehearsed the scene, choreographing the route that I should take through the trees, finding places to amplify each dramatic beat. We then rehearsed with the camera operator.

It was a joy to be able to play the whole thing through, as the momentum, the pace and the shape of the scene could really be

dictated by performance, almost like acting on stage. The adrenalin rush really puts you in the moment, knowing you have to rise to the occasion, because once you start a nearly three-minute scene, there's no going back. We shot the scene several times and then the camera operator had the phenomenally difficult job of matching the timing and the shot exactly, with me off camera performing the dialogue. With no actor in the frame the natural tendency would be to speed up, because it's so odd shooting an empty plate, but he matched it perfectly.

One of my favourite sets I got to work on was the Forbidden Pool. It was exactly as I had imagined it from the book, an amazing rock amphitheatre with a fully functioning waterfall dropping into a plunge pool. Sméagol is at his happiest, having banished the Gollum side of his personality and growing closer to Frodo. He has caught a fish so things are looking good. However, unbeknown to him, he is being watched by Faramir and his men. Stealing fish from this pool is punishable by death, and the archers are ready to execute him. High above the pool, Frodo confesses to Faramir that Sméagol is his guide, thereby saving him. He then calls Sméagol, who senses that something isn't quite right, but follows his master. Faramir's men capture the unsuspecting creature and take him away for interrogation.

> 'rock and pool
> is sweet and cool
> so nice for feet,
> we only wish
> to catch a fish
> so juicy sweet!'

I wanted to find a way of expressing this moment of relative happiness for Sméagol before the awful misunderstanding that Frodo has betrayed him. So I had the idea that he could be singing away to himself as he beat the fish on a rock. Peter and Fran liked the idea and so it went in. This scene was

eventually motion captured a year and a half after we shot on the set.

It's extraordinary to think that I only ever worked with two other actors apart from Sean and Elijah – Thomas Robbins and David Wenham, who played Faramir. David and I met briefly on the hilltops of Ithilien (Twelve Mile Delta in the South Island), but we only actually acted together in two scenes.

The first was at the entrance to the sewers of the besieged city of Osgiliath. It was early days for David, and I remember him dealing with all the technical challenges for the first time. By now we'd all grown accustomed to the myriad of different components that went into a single shot, but it can blow your mind coming into a world where for every single scene you need a performance pass with Gollum, one without, one with a scale

double for him ('Tall Paul' Randall), one with the scale doubles for Elijah and Sean (Fon and Kieran), another acting with Sean and Elijah on their knees, then having to do things like miming holding Gollum by the throat while I performed the voice off camera – all this and while acting as well! David had the lot all at once. Needless to say,

he nailed it *and* brought phenomenal depth to Gondor's ill-treated second son.

The second scene we played together was the interrogation of Sméagol by the Rangers at Henneth Annûn. Faramir wants to know where he and the Hobbits are travelling to in this time of war. Sméagol, who had been brutally kicked around like a football (in what Peter referred to as the *Clockwork Orange* scene), crawls into a corner of the cave and begins to mutter to himself. Gollum is convincing Sméagol that Frodo has betrayed them, that 'they stole it from us'. Faramir realises that they hold the key to saving his country, which would finally enable him to gain the respect of his father, Denethor (played by John Noble).

We played the scene with Gollum's back to camera, so only his sobbing and heaving could be seen through his body language as the internal debate raged. David was great to work with, and I loved watching his portrayal

of a man with such a great personal and political dilemma unfold.

The final scene I'd be working on before principal photography ended was to motion capture the rabbit scene. So out came my two furry friends again – and the suit with the reflective dots. Peter had cut the scene together, which meant that we could play the action through shot for shot. We were now getting into the swing of using motion capture. The joy of it is that things happen physically in the spur of the moment. A slight trip, a falter, a deep breath, all this body language is picked up and becomes part of the performance, giving it a greater sense of reality to the human eye. Getting used to doing it on my own was odd, having played the scene with the boys for real, but they were up there on screen, and it was only a matter of time before I got used to it. I got a huge amount of satisfaction

seeing the CG Gollum, interacting with Sean and Elijah, and I could begin to sense that this could be a really great way of working.

After being totally vegetarian for years and years, I finally started eating fish again— a result of feeling permanently tired, scares about processed soya being carcinogenic, and the array of fresh seafood on set. Is it the slippery slope? Will all my principles begin to tumble one by one until I'm a voracious red-blooded, war-mongering species supremacist? Gollum, I blame you. 'Give it to us raw and wriggling' indeed!.

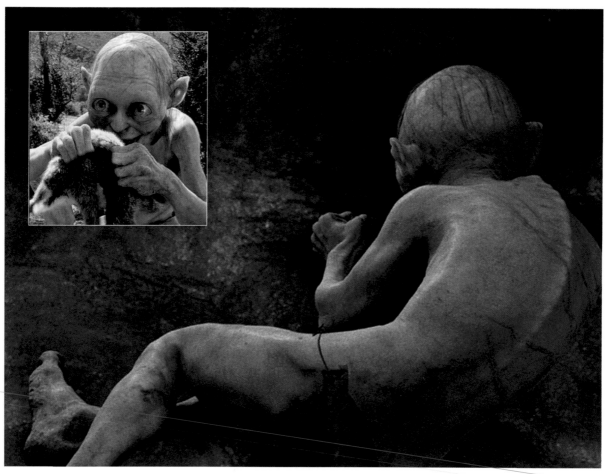

CHAPTER NINE
Escape from Middle-earth

We all participated in the very first press conference for the film in a tent next to the Minas Tirith set, and only local journalists were invited as a way of saying, 'Thank you Wellington – this is when it all started.' I remember John Rhys Davies telling the assembled press, 'This is going to be bigger than *Star Wars*,' which made everyone nervous, even though many of us actually believed he could be right.

Amazingly, we reached the end of principal photography in time for Christmas, with Pete calling it a wrap on 22 December 2000, on shedule. The wrap party was held in a huge warehouse down on the waterfront and was an incredible event. There were around 3,000 people who had worked on the production, all in one building celebrating the achievement. The cast performed a *haka*, there were great Kiwi bands playing, a huge food tent served culinary delights from around the globe, and an amazing out-takes compilation was screened. It was one hell of a night.

Two of our closest friends, Bev and Jhan, had flown over for the end of the shoot and to spend Christmas with us touring the South Island in a Maui camper bus. This six-berth bus would be our home for the next two and a half weeks, and we had a very ambitious itinerary planned: Ferry to Picton; drive to Abel Tasman National Park; Totranui; Greymouth gold mining town; drive down west coast to Fiordland; Fox Glacier; Queenstown; Dart River safari; Mount Cook; Hanmer Springs; Kaikoura.

I'm a bit of a hard taskmaster when it comes to expeditions, er, I mean holidays. All those years of climbing trips, and the preparation involved, plus the sheer adrenaline rush of going away to discover new wilderness, turns me into a complete control freak. I always try to do too much, and I think I was responsible for exhausting my family and friends as we tried to see every square inch of the South Island, but we did see Mount Cook on the one perfectly sunny day in weeks, and we saw whales at Kaikoura. Unforgettable.

Now the idea was that I'd remain in Wellington for about six weeks and complete all the motion capture and ADR, and that would be it – no more Gollum, *finito*. We would head back home to resume our lives, play new characters, move on.

WHAT WAS I THINKING? I don't know how that little plan was conceived, but it proved to be mere fantasy. Looking back now, in June 2003, when we're still shooting new scenes, I can't believe I was so naive. With the prospect of time on our hands, we decided to go on holiday to Fiji and have some quality family time. The day we were about to book the trip, I received a message from Sean Gascoine, my agent. I'd been offered the role of Factory Records producer, 'mad professor' Martin Hannett, in Michael Winterbottom's new film, *24 Hour Party People*.

Tough call. Long family summer holiday in sunny Fiji, or low-budget art movie in Manchester in the middle of winter? There's no contest.

As the train pulled into a grey Manchester Piccadilly station, freezing raindrops pierced my skull like icy needles, as if to say, 'Ha ha ha, you sucker! You're an actor, and you can't fight it.'

24 Hour Party People was crazy. Utter craziness. I did love playing Hannett, once I found him. He was a local legend, a real pioneer, a consumer of all things chemical – a chemist and musical alchemist. Bands loved and hated him according to his unpredictable mood swings. This film was the complete and utter antithesis of *The Lord of the Rings*, all shot loosely with handheld digital cameras, improvised, messy, chaotic. I actually wore trousers again! No crawling on all fours was involved.

Actually that's not true. Most of the cast crawled into work on all fours every day…

Next up was a low-budget never-to-be-seen prison drama, *The Escapist*, shot in Dublin in April, directed by Gillies MacKinnon and

starring Jonny Lee Miller, with yours truly playing psycho killer Ricky Barnes. I'd love to know where all these films we Brits make end up. There must be hundreds and hundreds of British films in a low-budget prison somewhere, serving life sentences.

That's why as an actor in the UK, if you can, you end up going back to the theatre. Because you get to flex your acting muscles,

work on a character, and are guaranteed that people will actually see you do your thing, which has got to be the point after all. Having a performance sitting in a can on a shelf waiting for distribution can really test your patience. So when I was offered the part of Jake in Sam Shepard's *A Lie of the Mind* at the Donmar Warehouse, directed by my good friend Wilson Milam, I couldn't refuse. Jake is a messed-up wife beater, who is in huge denial.

Hold on, can you spot the trend? Messed-up Ring junkie, messed-up musical genius junkie, messed-up psycho killer, messed-up wife beater… My mum keeps asking me when I'm going to play someone nice!

Anyway, 2001 was the year of investigating the dark side. So while I was in this frame of mind I decided to write and direct my own short film looking at the dark side of the British National Health system. It would be a comedy called *Snake*.

It had been quite some time since Gollum's voice had come out of my mouth and the character that I'd been playing, Jake, had a totally different vocal range, which my vocal chords had attuned to. So I was very nervous about the ADR I would be doing on *Fellowship* in August. Even though it was only a relatively small amount of

work, it was obviously crucial to get the throat working in the same way, as the voice would be the audience's main introduction to the character, more so than the images, which were purposely designed to keep him mysteriously in the shadows, until *The Two Towers*.

It was great to see Pete and Fran when I arrived at Pinewood Studios. They were in London recording the score with Howard Shore and also recording ADR for several of the cast. It always takes time to get back into a character when there's been a long break between filming and ADR, but this was particularly tricky and I felt very dislocated from him. There's always a moment when you think it's never going to come back as potently as when you first shot a scene, but you usually get over it.

Once the play was over, preparations to shoot *Snake* got underway. The story revolves around a young medical student (Rupert Graves) performing backstreet operations to pay for his medical education, a middle-aged man (Bev Willis) who's wife needs a kidney or she'll die, and a prostitute (Lorraine Ashbourne) who needs a hip operation so she can keep working. My producing partner Paul Viragh and I had temporary office space in a basement in Soho care of our executive, John Tadros, and the project became more ambitious than I'd originally planned, with friends throughout the industry offering their talents. One morning I was in the office trying to blag a camera crane for this particular shot I wanted to do, when one of the staff leant over and said, 'Andy, look at this!' I looked on his computer, which was showing CNN News, to see a very pixellated shot of a plane flying into the World Trade Centre in New York.

Osama Bin Laden, allegedly living in a cave under the mountains in a country far away, was deemed the man responsible for the attack on the Twin Towers, and the fierce desire to purge the world of evil first became a reality when American forces began to bomb Afghanistan, assisting the Northern Alliance in their attempt to overthrow the Taliban regime. I'll never forget seeing a haunting photograph of a Taliban soldier who had been left by the wayside after his comrades had retreated. A group of Northern Alliance troops had stripped him of his clothes, beaten him, and dragged him along a rubble road. The look in his eyes was that of a hunted animal. I couldn't help connecting that image to the one of Gollum being beaten up by the Rangers.

Friends of mine were buying gas masks, hoarding bottled water, panicking about travelling into London by tube, unable to look up at a plane in the sky, checking their mail for anthrax. It was a strange time. We were all paralysed by apocalyptic fear, and yet we tried to carry on as normal.

18 December 2001

The opening of *The Fellowship of the Ring* was quite something. The speculation was over. The world no longer had to wait, and the premiere at the Odeon Leicester Square in London was indeed a major event. Peter got up on stage to rapturous applause and introduced the cast one by one. Because Gollum would really make his first major appearance in *The Two Towers* and was being kept secret, I hadn't been involved in the press

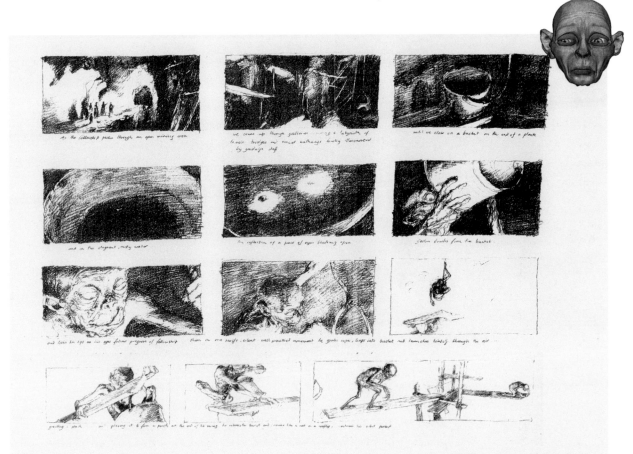

Alan Lee's storyboard for a Gollum sequence that didn't make it into The Fellowship of the Ring

tour, and hadn't even seen the film until that night. As the lights went down, my heart was racing. When it was over I was so overwhelmed by the emotional power and magnitude of film that I sat in my seat, next to my dear friend and agent Lou Coulson, completely drained by the experience. I mean, I'd been there and witnessed the filming of it. I could barely find the words to tell Peter and Fran how extraordinary it was. There aren't many films in one's life that have this kind of impact. I started to realise how much work needed to be done on Gollum over the course of the next year.

On New Year's Eve, Lorraine and I vowed to each other that this year we'd finally get married. It was going to be a mission. But where, how, why? We'd been together for years, we had children, so we wanted to find our own way of marking our partnership. I'd always wanted us to get married on top of a mountain, so we went to the Lake District, where we'd spent our early courting days. Unfortunately we were all hit by a stomach bug and spent every day in a hotel room, while it rained relentlessly outside.

The search would have to continue once I returned from my next trip inside the unstable mind of my alter ego, Gollum, who was calling me from Wellington to go back I knew that this year was going to be 'make or break' time for the little fella.

CHAPTER TEN

The Changing Face of Gollum

Since I'd been away there had been some significant changes. Since I was playing young Sméagol as well, Peter had decided that he wanted the facial structure of Gollum to resemble mine much more

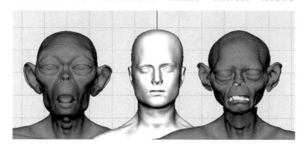

closely, and also so that the CG muscles would be capable of replicating the range of facial expressions that originated from my performance. Christian Rivers had originally instigated the idea of this change of look, which Peter and Fran then developed with Bay Raitt. The final facial sculpts were to keep changing and being refined until quite late on. Also Gino was developing a paint scheme with Joe Letteri, to give the skin layers and textures.

A lot of the Gollum illustrations I'd seen before the movies were from previous calendars and books and games and things, and had made him into a very froggy, amphibian sort of character — maybe people get that from the description in the book. Before we started designing our Gollum we thought it was important for our story that Frodo could become like Gollum, as Gollum started out as a Hobbit-like creature. Should Frodo fail in his quest, should he fail to give up the Ring, should the Ring overpower him, then he had a very direct pathway to becoming the same sort of creature that Gollum is. Therefore the froggy, amphibian thing didn't really serve us, so we started to design the Gollum you see briefly in The Fellowship of the Ring *— Gollum Mark One, I call him.*

Andy started out being just the voice but he was physically changing himself into Gollum and giving a full-blooded performances that was the way he found the voice — it was the process that Andy went through. Even though Gollum was going to be a CG character, we were seeing a flesh and blood person actually acting the role and I thought it would be incredibly valuable for Elijah Wood and Sean Astin to have Andy there on set as a visual reference.

When we started work on the Two Towers shots of Gollum, we found we wanted to replicate Andy's performance as much as we could with the CG character. However, we found that we couldn't — Andy's basic facial structure, his muscles, eyes, cheeks, mouth and his performance — weren't the same as we had built into our CG Gollum. Yet we wanted Gollum to look like Andy, so when Andy used the muscles of his face and created an expression, the CG character could create that same look. At that point it became obvious that if we were going to use Andy's performances as reference, we were going to have to rebuild our CG Gollum face.

Peter Jackson, Director

I thought that Gollum, basically, should have been a very easy concept to nail down. He is kind of thin, sinewy, maybe not emaciated but quite drawn, with big eyes and balding, long hair and a few teeth missing. Turning that into a character took a long time, especially back in 1998 before Andy had been cast. We went through pencil drawings, maquettes, design after design. Even after the shooting had finished we were still redesigning him, because the films evolved as they were being made.

Then Pete cast Andy for the voice, and then got him to actually perform as Gollum in a lot of the shots, which we then had to mimic through digital animation. Then he cast him as Sméagol and we looked again at our design and realised the character we'd done was completely incongruous to Andy as Sméagol. It didn't look anything like him! So, we went back and redesigned him, keeping all those initial concepts but imagining that Gollum could evolve from Andy. I tried to keep the proportions similar but incorporate a lot more of Andy's facial features. So, rather than having that little turned up button nose, I gave him a bit more of an angular nose, lips based on a thinner version of Andy's, and though Gollum's eyes are dramatically large, I tried to keep a lot of the angles of the brow the same. And it is a lot more effective, because now we've merged all those elements together, hopefully when people watch it they're wondering if it's a puppet, CG, or if it's a freaky actor in make-up.

Christian Rivers, Designer, Weta Digital

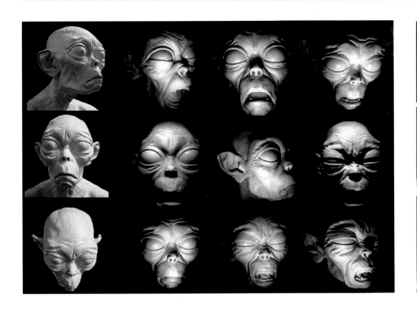

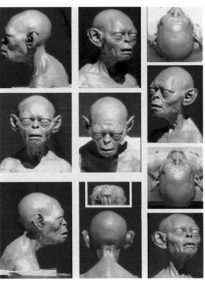

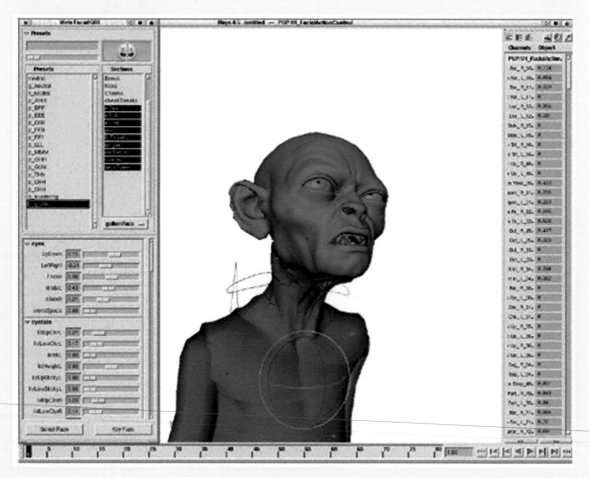

A conversation I had in 1999 changed my life. Charlie McClellan, then the producer for Weta Digital, was recruiting people to work on the special effects for the trilogy. We were talking in a hotel room somewhere in LA, wondering about how this tiny company in the South Pacific was planning to pull off the one of the biggest effects projects of all time.

I sat on a small couch thumbing a set of software manuals I had helped write. I was calm. I had a good job, working with people I believed in. I was at this interview because my mom read me Tolkien as a kid, and so I had to see if I was to be a part of it. I remember thinking that if these guys didn't sound like they had vision, I would walk out. I would hope that if they managed to finish the movies, they wouldn't insult the books too much.

A white-haired New Zealander, looking more than a bit like the actor Rutger Hauer, was outlining how he saw the CG setup at Weta coming into existence. John Sheils, the pre-production digital supervisor, believed in what he was saying, and to my growing apprehension, he was starting to make sense. After watching an impressive pre-production demo reel made by Weta Digital, I asked the question that sent me packing across the seas to New Zealand. 'This all looks really cool, but

how are you going to do Gollum's face?' Charlie replied, 'We were hoping you could take care of that.'

Two and a half years later, just before Christmas, Peter Jackson, with a slew of Weta Digital folks standing around a conference table, slowly spun a clay sculpture of Gollum's head around on a turntable. After a few moments he looked at me and asked what I thought. 'I think this design will have more emotive range and will play better against Sam and Frodo,' I said. And he nodded and said 'Go!' Workshop sculptor Jamie Beswarick and I grabbed it and ran out of the room. I think more than a few people were laughing at us because with less than a few months to go before full production, it had just been decided to redesign Gollum's face. Tensions were a little high because this meant that no Gollum shots could start until my team and I finished rebuilding his facial system.

Jamie and I ran through the building laughing. We grabbed a camera from the camera department and ran out into the parking lot to take reference photos of it. Getting a team together to help build Gollum's face was tricky. Fairly early on we decided that if we were to keep Gollum consistent, we were going to need to clearly define his emotional range using only a few digital artists rather than a team of fifty and even if we did end up with fifty animators working on Gollum, he would always need to feel like he was the same person. We wanted to avoid the situation where each animator was defining the character on a shot-by-shot basis based on their skill level. Gollum needed to be consistent in the same way as a flesh and blood actor would be. And, just as with a real actor, we had to define things his face could and couldn't do. We didn't want him warping from his cousin to his brother to his grampa – he had to be Gollum the whole time.

To do this, Francouis LaRoche, Jason Schleifer, Jeff Hameluck and I defined a 'facial expression volume', within which we would be able to constrain all the animation for Gollum's face – in other words, we could keep it consistent.

It sounds complicated, and it is. But the basics of the system involves an artform I've come to call 'combination sculpting'. If you imagine all the nerves in your face and all their combinations, you

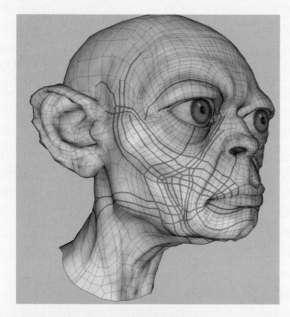

can understand why Gollum has over 900 combination shapes. And why, I'm somewhat ashamed to say, I sculpted over 10,000 individual facial expressions while designing the nerve control structure we would finally use for him.

To get the redesign done on time meant that that I had to find three digital sculptors who could assist me. They needed to be fast, talented, rock-solid sculptors. Andy Serkis was to be our guide, but Gollum was certainly not human. I needed folks who could sculpt and draw without reference, and would know how to caricature. Combination sculpting is like traditional cel animation, except that each drawing has to look good from every angle and the sequence must make sense in any order. I needed 3D pixel ninjas! After looking through hundreds of resumes and portfolios, John Feather and Sven Jensen along with Bradfod deCaussin from Weta's modelling department joined the Gollum facial team.

While I was madly trying to get the final model approved, Brad, Sven and John practised using the combination sculpting system I had set up. Each of them went through a period of intense 'brain sweat' while they were trying to figure it out. Understanding how to balance skin distribution, subsurface form, and animation flexibility without making it look bland is a tall order. I'd had two years to invent, refine, practise and absorb the design aesthetic of Gollum, and I was asking these guys to suck it all in in a month.

I was really worried that it wasn't going to sink in, and that I had simply gone off on a fools' errand building a system that was too crazy to attempt to rebuild in such a short time. But the guys came through.

I remember each of them having this moment where they just stared at their monitors thinking about what I was asking them to do. They would make some minuscule change, compile a face and then laugh and turn to me and say something along the lines of, 'This is so cool, Bay!'

I think that was the highlight of my experience on The Lord of the Rings. Well, maybe that and the night at the premiere when the audience stopped laughing after Gollum calls Sméagol a murderer. Or maybe the first time I saw the Cave Troll's snarl in Balin's tomb with the music and sound – OK, there a lot of highlights.

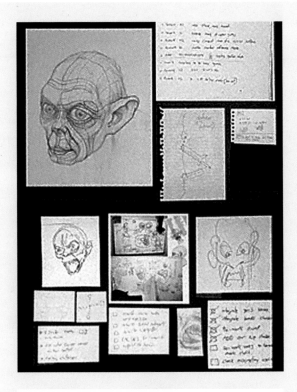

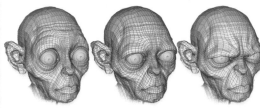

One weekend Weta had to have all the power turned off, so I brought my computers back to my house. Sven was with me, and we worked through the weekend. Sven had hit some snag with a particular Gollum expression and was really frustrated, so we started talking about it at length, and then, sometime around 3 a.m., we hit a 'Eureka!' moment. We figured out how to make Gollum's sneer, frown and squints work perfectly and by 7 a.m. we had what we call a shape network which made the shot for the line, 'What does it call me?' just sing. The way Gollum dropped his face in that is a direct result of that frustrated late-night conversation.

I think one the most intense things about doing this job was getting to work with all the animators. Randy Cook, the animation director, was a mentor and leader for us all. His skills as a draughtsman, animator and sculptor are nothing short of incredible − he could look at what I was trying to do with a shape network, and make the subtlest comment that would make the whole thing buzz with presence.

The size of Gollum's eyes caused me the most grief. Peter Jackson always wanted the eyes bigger, and the animators always wanted them smaller. Every time the eyes were changed it meant a lot of reworking for me. From the design side, it makes a lot of sense, but from the animation side, too much eye-whites can make the expression seem unclear. I was often the no-can-do guy for the animators − I felt it was my job to support them and what they had to do, and I always felt bad whenever an animator wanted something that was outside the scope of what we had defined for Gollum. We did keep refining Gollum right up to the end of The Return of the King, but each time we changed it, the animators had to re-learn it. It was sort of like a piano builder swapping new variations out from under a concert pianist trying to practise for a show. The animators were incredibly forgiving of all the construction we were doing around them.

Bay Raitt, Creature Facial Lead, Weta Digital

The methodology of creating Gollum was really starting to firm up. As *The Two Towers* was beginning to take shape in the cutting room, Peter was making selects (or shot choices) in the Gollum scenes which were dictated by the performance, and then choosing the right technical route to support that decision. Peter insisted that the footage we'd shot on set be placed side by side on the animators' computer screens next to their CG Gollum, so that the performance could be closely followed.

Three main approaches were taken: *Rotoscoping, Key-frame animation* and *Motion capture.*

In the fight sequence between Gollum, Frodo and Sam, Pete wanted to use the takes where I actually was on screen fighting, with my body wrapped around Sean's as he struggled to break free, to ensure the energy and contact felt real, and so the painstaking method of rotoscoping was employed. The roto-artists literally drew in Gollum's skinny body over my exact movements and then painted out the excess fat (me) frame by frame. It was very time-consuming, precise procedure, but nevertheless, the right choice for the shot.

This method was used in many instances, such as when Sméagol is grasping Frodo's cloak whilst persuading him not to enter Mordor through the Black Gates, and again when Gollum pulls Frodo out of the water in the Dead Marshes.

Key frame animation was used in certain sections of scenes, using the performance on set as a guide (for instance the opening shot of Gollum being dragged by the rope in Emyn Muil). It was also used at times when it was physically impossible to actually perform on the terrain, such as the first shot of Gollum crawling down the vertical rock face while the Hobbits are asleep. Most importantly, the face was key-frame animated.

In acting terms, facial expressions are an outward manifestation of internal emotions. What the animators did with that set of acting impulses was to translate them on to the muscle structure of the Gollum puppet.

By now Bay Raitt had worked on the evolution of Gollum's facial structure over a long period of time. When I saw the final Gollum sculpture, I was totally amazed. I told Bay that it looked like a cross between my father and my son: Gollum was like my father, and Sméagol was like my son. The muscles could be controlled by faders and were arranged into key poses representing a wide range of emotional states. Once this was done, the animators could return to the performance I had originally given on set and on the motion capture stage. Peter would choose specific takes that he wanted matched identically (for instance in the central schizophrenic scene), otherwise the animators took the essence of a performance and amplified it. We would then collaborate further by making sure each beat was working correctly, and if necessary I could act out sections of scenes in one-on-one sessions with the animators to fine-tune specific looks or moments.

Most importantly since *Fellowship*, Peter wanted to use motion capture on a much greater scale. Many scenes were shot again in this way, directed by Peter, Fran, Philippa or

I like actors. I like acting. I like performance and I like animation – love them all. But I always thought that animated characters in live action movies, and I'm sure Peter feels this way too, were often achieved by the use of animation solutions rather than acting solutions. When I read Tolkien's book in the 1960s, I thought what a great and probably impossible-to-do stop-motion character Gollum would be. As computers came in to enhance puppetry, there were always new solutions being developed by people like Rick Baker, where you can actually computer control a character's face.

Basically our challenge – or our desire, we never saw it as a challenge – was always to put, through animation, an acting performance on screen which was appropriate to the scene. The character had to have the same level of reality that all the other characters in the film had. His acting style had to be sympathetic with the acting style of all the other players in the ensemble, because although Gollum is a star turn, he's also part of an ensemble and he's a dramatic character, so aside from all the obvious technical challenges and needs that had to be met in making him believable, one had to also be aware what the character was thinking.

All our animators had to have the same understanding of the character that Andy did. If they were merely copying him, tracing him uncomprehendingly, something would be missing because then they

would become not actors but impressionists. An imitation of a famous person by an impressionist, no matter how much it sounds like him, is still just an impression, and often exaggerated and unreal.

Although the look was predetermined by Richard's team at Weta Workshop, and, of course, by Peter's influence, as far as how the character behaved, that had a lot to do with us. Mike Stevens did something with Gollum at one point that wasn't based on Andy's work at all, making him very tactile, almost coquettish, really creepy. I'd never have thought of that but it's a cool route to go down, kind of twisted and scary.

Just as a bigger movement is more interesting to animate than a guy sitting in a chair nodding, so a bigger performance is more fun to do than something that's understated. But while anyone can play, say, Caligula, not everyone can play him well. Something can be huge and a real crowd-pleaser yet wrong ultimately for the spirit of the character and the movie. So I tried to fight against any sort of theatrical cheapness, doing something that's entertaining but wrong, and out of character. I don't think Gollum's meant to be a totally understated character, but it was sometimes quite a fine line between something big and true and big and all over the place. He has to be extreme, he has to be a Caligula, but it's got to be beautifully performed, unique to himself. That's the challenge that I hope we met – to make him unique, different, not like every villain you've ever seen, every monster or drug addict you've ever seen. Andy and I talked about this when we first met, because I always saw Gollum being an addict. We discussed it and Andy had come to the same conclusion on his own. It's a pretty obvious and I think accurate hook to hang the performance on, because it's the corruption by power – he's at war with himself, and has manifested several distinct sides that are actual separate identities.

Villains are awfully easy to play and the more lovable they are the better. Gollum's got to be legitimately sympathetic, but he's also an interesting villain. He's a real meaty character, and I hope that the emotions will be conflicting about what's happened to this guy.

Randall William Cook, Animation Design Supervisor

Randy, and it was here that we were able to hone Gollum's performance without the pressure of shooting on film, sometimes sticking closely to what was shot on set and other times reinventing it. The beauty of motion capture is that it is very sensitive and can pick up very subtle movement such as breathing and also incidental movement such as a stumble, adding reality in rooting the character to its environment, which greatly helped in playing the painful effort of Gollum's movement.

Traditionally, animated characters tend to be busy on screen, as animators have felt the necessity to fill every frame with business. Unlike a conventional screen performance, there's hardly ever a moment of reflection or repose.

What we were all beginning to realise was that when you watch great screen acting, the majority of emotion and internalised thought is obviously conveyed through the eyes. Gollum had to be able to be still, have moments of great stillness, and let the

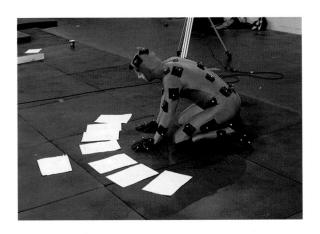

audience in – he had to be able to 'carry a close-up' in the same way Elijah and Sean could. It's interesting looking back at some of the earlier scenes I did, because they were much more demonstrative and melodramatic, busy and at times over-energised. This was partly due to the fact that I was exaggerating the emotions of the character, to show the animators what Gollum was feeling, whereas in the later performances I was more aware that I could internalise the feelings and still be confident that it was reading to the viewer.

The mocap unit had also transformed from the early pioneering days in to a fully

We wanted to recreate what is compelling about a human performance. If you look at close-ups of actors, it is all down to very subtle facial movements and their eyes. In one shot sad and one happy, while there's no visible difference on the actor's face, you can tell what the emotion is in the eyes. The emotion that they're playing basically comes from their soul, and computers don't have souls. That, to me, was the real secret we had to crack with Gollum. We had to analyse physically what we can do to recreate that on an artificial level. We couldn't afford to have it look artificial – it had to look totally real.

Peter Jackson, Director

operational crew working in a swish new hi-tech environment. Remington Scott (who had created the first fully mocapped animation feature, *Final Fantasy*) was now supervisor, and members of the mocap software team were on hand to work through technical problems. Lisa Wildermoth was the first assistant director.

I began overseeing the motion capture production for The Two Towers *in January 2002. With less than ten months of production until the delivery deadline for the visual effects, I was responsible for over 12,000 motions for the massive battle sequences. The work that we were doing for these shots comprised tens of thousands of characters interacting with each other, and I think of it as a thunderous symphony of human kinematics in action. This was the visual equivalent of a deafening orchestra featuring thousands of instruments playing simultaneously.*

However, more daunting than that was the challenge of motion capturing and integrating the most ambitious hyper-real principal computer generated character in film. This one lone character had the emotional, psychological and physical depth of one of the most complex personalities in literary history. If the massive hordes could be thought of as an orchestra, then I think of this personality as a solo instrumentalist whose haunting notes linger in solitude. My responsibility was to ensure that Gollum would be a completely unique character driven by the sole performance of Andy Serkis.

There were three motion capture productions with Andy. The first consisted of two week-long capture sessions in late January/early February 2002, the second was in June for two weeks and the third was a week in July.

To ensure that Peter Jackson could direct Gollum as if he were an actor on the set during production rather than as a post-production computer animated character, it was essential to see Andy's performance retargeted to Gollum in real-time. In order to do this we had to design special charmaps (character maps) that allowed for the offset of Andy's joints to the disproportionate skeleton of Gollum. James van der Reyden, motion capture lead technician, designed several charmaps for different actions; when Andy was performing on his feet, when he was on his knees, and when he crawled on his hands and feet. Later, the motion editors would blend between these charmaps when Gollum's actions changed between bipedal and quadruped.

With all of this working, Peter had the ability to view on a monitor the retargeted captured actions of Andy as the CG Gollum in real-time. This was a truly flexible pipeline that allowed Peter to be able to make changes or modify the capture accordingly, and he did. He used every variation we gave him to push the limits of the medium to ensure that we recorded Andy's motion exactly as was needed to convey the action, personality and emotion of Gollum for each shot.

Three video operators, who were remotely stationed at the periphery of the capture zone, recorded each take simultaneously. The video provided a close-up, medium and wide shot of Andy's action to be used as expression reference for the animation department. Each camera was also recorded as a separate track and was played back for Peter's review.

Sean Mathiesen, motion capture technician, worked on the night shift recording the selected takes on to miniDV disk. Each take was recorded against the plate and with a blue background. These takes were then rushed over to editorial so Peter could cut them into the film and decide the exact frame ranges for each shot. These selects were also used for reference for Andy's final voice sessions.

We had over eight hours of refined and edited motion capture of Gollum from which Peter chose the final actions. Many of the shots featuring Gollum that were integrated and edited to approval were ultimately cut from the theatrical print. However, I'm looking forward to seeing these scenes restored in the extended DVD.

The power of motion capture, as demonstrated through Andy's performance, is one in which an actor can expand beyond traditional typecasting and play a character that is completely different in physical appearance. This is pushing the boundaries of film technology and the relationship between the actor and audience.

Remington Scott, Motion Capture Supervisor

I was upgraded to a shiny blue suit that was less gimp more speed-skater in appearance. There was an additional crew of three video camera operators, filming the performances for reference, and a sound crew experimented with recording live sound as we did the mocap. What this all amounts to is that, when Peter and Fran walked in on the first day's shooting, there was a real sense of 'let's get down to business'.

The main three scenes we motion captured during this block were Emyn Muil (Gollum swearing to serve the master of the 'precious'), the Black Gate (Gollum secretly reliving his memory of torture on top of the rocky bluff), and sections of the Dead Marshes, (Gollum leading the Hobbits through bogs full of corpses). For the first time a strange phenomenon took place. We were actually

The motion capture department is unique at Weta Digital in that we get to work closely with real human performers. Lucky for us, but very difficult for the performer who has no costume, make-up, physical set or props to get him into character.

In Andy's case it was even harder as he had to act scenes he had shot months, sometimes years earlier on the live set, without the other actors who had been with him in those scenes – often he would act against a rubber head on a stick. It's amazing that anyone could give a good performance under these conditions, but Andy always gave a remarkable one. At times he had the crew in tears, which is astounding considering what a bunch of cynics we are. Other times I've had to sternly tell the crew not to laugh during a take, which we all know not to, but they just couldn't help themselves.

Gollum has become my favourite character in the movies. I do realise that as a Weta Digital person I am biased, but I can't help it. Andy was one of my favourite actors to work with – capturing him was always a pleasure, his graciousness toward the crew universally acknowledged. Gollum is such a complex character; he evokes both sympathy and abhorrence at the same time. The casting of Andy for Gollum was either incredibly good luck or shows how very, very clever Peter Jackson and Fran Walsh are.

Lisa Wildermoth, *First Assistant Director, Mocap*

originating new scenes in the motion capture studio, which would then be shot on film with Elijah and Sean *afterwards*. It felt like the technology was finally bowing to the creative possibility, and that was a joyous departure. In many ways I think this was my happiest, most exhilarating time of the whole project, when at last there was a real uninterrupted flow of creative energy. I was working very intensively, discovering new things in the character every day, and working directly with Pete and Fran with whom I felt totally in sync.

There was also a new routine. We'd shoot motion capture one day and then the next day we'd ADR the scene we'd just mocapped, so it was fresh and recent. We then had the flexibility to experiment further with dialogue before it would be selected and all sent down to Weta Digital for the animators to take the baton.

It was at this time that Fran and I sat down to work out a new road map for Gollum's journey in *The Two Towers*. Fran, Philippa and I were all aware that although the character was functioning on a level, there was a way to go before he really dramatically impacted on the whole story, and most importantly on the developing relationship with Frodo.

We also worked on the dramatic reasoning behind his 'schizophrenia'. This was probably the most crucial stage of his development. In

Since the end of principal photography for the trilogy, the mocap crew have had the privilege of watching Andy weave his magic on the mocap stage. Through the process, the team and techniques have evolved as much as the character of Gollum.

Although we capture the raw motion of Gollum, it is the combination of the skills from every department within Weta Digital, and several different software programmes, that takes the brilliant performances from Andy and brings Gollum to life on screen.

It was a first for us to have a principal actor and the director work together on our stage. Suffice to say, we were very nervous that first day, although it was wonderful to see Andy Serkis and Peter Jackson working together. We were initially scheduled to capture 12 shots but after Peter had seen the possibilities, we ended up capturing 112 shots in the first Gollum block! We also found it pretty intimating to be suddenly inundated with all the crew that comes as part and parcel of working with a principal actor and director. Our normal crew numbers six or seven, plus an actor or stunt performer. Suddenly we averaged about 20 to 25 people on set.

Andy's dedication to the Gollum character is inspiring. It wasn't uncommon to find all the crew emotionally moved by his performances – an art in itself, when you realise this is a guy in a blue Lycra suit, moving around a set that looks nothing like the background on the video monitor, acting on his own. Because of Andy's exceptional work ethic we were able to evolve the process to the point where it would be disturbing to most actors – we feel that most actors of his quality wouldn't be able to endure the rigours of working within a virtual reality. We also greatly admired Andy's ability to make everyone instantly feel like his friend, and he quickly made himself part of the mocap crew. During the first block of Gollum capture we did not have a green room so we hired a trailer for him, identical to those used on principal photography. Andy only went to it once, briefly, for all of about five seconds, and then only because someone mentioned the bet that was on that he wouldn't use it at all! He was much happier hanging out on the floor with everyone.

It is sad to know that the end is in sight for Gollum and the mocap crew. Working with Andy has been a true privilege. We feel honoured to have been involved in the process, and we will miss him.

Frank Cowlrick
James van der Reyden
Jake Botting
Emily Pearce
Mahria Sangster
Lisa Wildermoth
John Curtis
David Bawel

between motion capture sessions we'd head back to Fran and Pete's house, where Fran had set up a board on which were pinned possible scene ideas and character notes. We began to formulate the idea that the Sméagol part of his personality, the younger naive side, had been squashed and diminished by the aggressive, pragmatic, vengeful Gollum part of his psyche, rather like a young child being abused by a controlling parent. Gollum had psychologically battered Sméagol into submission, so that he was almost lost forever.

Then Fran came up with the defining idea that this terrified Sméagol child could re-emerge through his growing connection and trust with Frodo, so that a fierce internal battle would really begin to grow, with Gollum being 'outed' and replaced by a new master. Sméagol could remember who he was again, feeling emotionally free from the hideous shackles that Gollum had kept him in, and

could, by talking to someone else apart from his Gollum self, find a kind of peace. This would also feed into Frodo's growing compassion and understanding of the weight of Sméagol's addiction and pain. As he helps Sméagol to reveal himself, Frodo learns to show pity and mercy, because he truly is beginning to sense the power that the Ring is having over himself. He needs to save Sméagol to know he can save himself. He is almost looking at a vision of himself, but much sicker.

I started to think of Gollum/Sméagol as a sufferer of a severe terminal illness in its latter stages of development, whilst Frodo is just coming to terms with having contracted the same disease. This connection, of course, is a complete anathema to Sam, who remains defiant that it is all a ploy for Gollum to get the Ring.

I was told at this time we'd be experimenting with the possibility of using facial motion

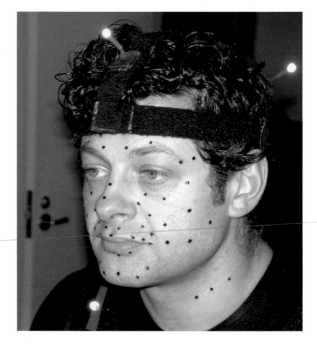

capture, which sounded very exciting. The thought that my facial expressions could drive the CG Gollum face as well as the body seemed to be the next logical step. One has to remember that this kind of technology was developing all the time, and it felt as if I were test-driving a new machine.

Remington Scott said, 'Hey Andy, check this out!' I was handed a photocopied colour picture of an actor in a tuxedo, and next to him an identical picture of the same actor. I looked at it for a while, but wasn't quite sure why.

'Sorry, Remington I don't get it, what is it?'

'Well, the guy on the right is the real actor and the guy on the left is CG. There's been some testing in LA with an actor playing a scene with himself using facial capture. We'd like to try to do this with Gollum.'

A clear plastic mask with little holes drilled in it was placed over my face, so that a make-up pencil could be poked through, leaving precisely measured dots all over my face. Each dot, like the dots on the body suit, was assigned to a particular or group of muscles so that the movements could be tracked. Just when I thought I couldn't possibly look any more ridiculous, I was now looking like I had a rare form of pox – and this became part of the everyday ritual during this motion capture shoot.

On one particular day, I sat in a chair with my facial dots, plus heavy eyeliner and bright red lipstick to accentuate the movements of eyes and lips (Marilyn Manson would have been terrified) and we shot all the scenes from *The Two Towers* in one sitting, using three cameras from different angles. This was going to be used by the animators to build a visual reference library of all the facial expressions I was using. It felt pretty sterile and scientific doing the performance this way, unable to be freed up physically because of having to sit in the chair, but I guess it was more a case of seeing how the face moved than using the energy of a fully acted performance.

After much discussion about whether to go down the facial capture route it was decided that there wasn't going to be enough time to get the system functioning quickly enough before the film's deadline, and in the end it was not pursued after all and Gollum's face would be key-frame animated.

Oh, the tempestuous marriage of animation and motion capture. I love them both but sometimes I feel that they are at war with each other and I'm in the middle. I can never understand it, aren't we all working towards the same goal — to make Gollum the most engaging CG character in a live action film? It's enough to drive a cyber-actor nuts! Sometimes they are like Gollum/Sméagol themselves.

Anim: *We hates mocap doesn't we preciousss?*

Moc: *Not Listening, Not listening.*

Anim: *Where would you be without ME? You exist because of ME!*

Moc: *Andy is our friend!*

Anim: *You don't have any friends, nobody likes YOU!*

Moc: *Go away and leave us to technically evolve, we don't need you any more.*

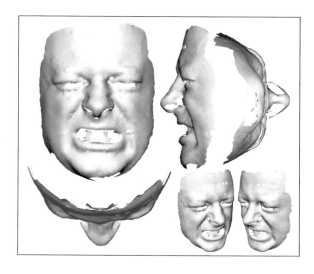

It was a very weird sensation. I remember going to the bathroom, during a mocap session, and looking at myself in the mirror. I didn't see me in the reflection. I felt as if I was moving like the CG Gollum. I lifted my hand to my face — it felt like Gollum's hand — I had transported myself physically into him. I know it sounds sensational but that is the only way to describe it. It's a very intense way of working and my brain hadn't processed coming out of it. This feeling stayed with me for some time.

I grabbed the chance of getting away from it all and caught the ferry across the water to the South Island. It was a wonderful trip, and made even more special because a huge pod of dolphins followed us all the way into Marlborough Sounds, a higgledy-piggledy formation of coves, bays and islands through which you weave your way towards Picton harbour where the ferry trip ends.

I stayed at a very laidback place called The Lazy Fish, which was only accessible by a small boat, and I spent two days walking the stunning Queen Charlotte track, which trails through lush forests and overlooks the sounds. It was actually on this trek that I first really considered the idea of writing this book, mainly because I wanted to share the experiences that I'd had on board this huge trilogy of films, as well as the filming experience itself. Whatever I did during my time away from work seemed to echo and enrich what was happening to the life and growth of the character.

So, motion capture was over for this block, we'd all learnt a hell of a lot and captured a phenomenal amount of shots, and the little grey-shaded Gollum was now continuing his pixellated odyssey into motion-editing before being handed over to animation. The next time I would be seeing the scenes we'd shot would be in a couple of months, when he'd have layers of skin and a

fully mobile and expressive face instead of a motionless, eyeless skull.

Mahria Sangstar, mocap co-ordinator, organised a mini short film festival for anyone to show some of their own work. The event took place at the cinema at Camper-down, and I was able to screen *Snake*, which was its first public showing. The place was packed. It's at times like this when you really do feel part of a massive extended family. There were some fantastically witty and far-out films, as well as spoofs, and it all re-affirmed what a monumental amount of talent and creativity there is thriving under *The Rings'* umbrella.

Back home for a couple of weeks in February, Lorraine and I were invited to the BAFTA Awards in London, where *Fellowship* scored very highly, including being voted best film by the public. After meetings about future projects, we went to LA for the Screen Actors Guild Awards, for which the cast had been nominated for best ensemble.

And then it was back to New Zealand for reshoots and new scenes for *The Two Towers*…

I remember the night the Oscar nominations were made. It was nearly 1.00 a.m. when I arrived at Pete and Fran's house. Executive producer Mark Ordesky was there, as were Philippa, and Chris and Dan Hennah. It was unbelievably thrilling as one by one the nominations came in, building to a staggering thirteen, and we all giggled and cheered as they were called out. Next to *Titanic*, *Fellowship* had scored the highest number of nominations ever in the history of the Academy.

Best Motion Picture of the Year
THE LORD OF THE RINGS:
THE FELLOWSHIP OF THE RING

Achievement in Directing
PETER JACKSON

Screenplay Based on Material Previously Produced or Published
FRAN WALSH, PHILIPPA BOYENS
& PETER JACKSON

Performance by an Actor
in a Supporting Role
IAN MCKELLEN

Achievement in Cinematography
ANDREW LESNIE

Achievement in Film Editing
JOHN GILBERT

Achievement in Sound
CHRISTOPHER BOYENS, MICHAEL SEMANICK,

GETHIN CREAGH & HAMMOND PEEK
Achievement in Art Direction
Art Direction: GRANT MAJOR
Set Decoration: DAN HENNAH

Achievement in Music in Connection
with Motion Pictures (Original Score)
HOWARD SHORE

Achievement in Visual Effects
JIM RYGIEL, RANDALL WILLIAM COOK, RICHARD TAYLOR &
MARK STETSON

Achievement in Costume Design
NGILA DICKSON & RICHARD TAYLOR

Achievement in Makeup
PETER OWEN & RICHARD TAYLOR

Achievement in Music in Connection
with Motion Pictures (Original Song)
"MAY IT BE" - Music and Lyric by
ENYA, NICKY RYAN & ROMA RYAN

CHAPTER ELEVEN

'Nobody likes you...'

The 'arc' or emotional journey of Sméagol/Gollum in *The Two Towers* had now been worked out. Fran and Philippa had worked through every line and re-assigned some dialogue that had been Sméagol to Gollum and vice versa. Now it was time to get together all the visual effects departments, including the animators, and talk through the progression of the character through the whole film. Traditionally, and I don't believe

When I first told people I wanted to work on The Lord of the Rings, *many people thought I was crazy. 'Why do you want to fly halfway around the world when you could get a good animation job here?' Honestly? It was because of Gollum. In my mind, he is one of the richest, most dynamic characters an animator could ever work on. But it wasn't all a bed of roses. We fought very hard to make him believable and I have some great memories of dailies review sessions and rigging meetings where people were bickering over the most minuscule things. But it was because of that dedication and passion that Gollum turned out as well as he did.*

Animators usually have a lot more creative control with their characters than we had on Gollum. I had to get used to the fact that Gollum was not mine, he belonged to Andy Serkis, Fran Walsh and, of course, Peter Jackson. After a while however it started to become clear that Gollum was actually starting to belong to himself. I was always partial to Sméagol and so I tried very hard to work on shots that were very clearly Sméagol. There was something very lovable in his pathetic need to please Frodo; he so wanted to have the trust of another living being – I always wanted to believe that there was good in him.

Technically, it was challenging because not only did we have to match our performance to Andy's, we had to navigate a myriad of interpretations of what that performance truly depicted. We would do shots over and over to get it right. It was frustrating at times, but I don't regret a moment of it. He was one of those characters I feel I could have worked on for a lifetime and only scratched the surface of his real depth.

Melanie Cordan,
Creature Designer, Weta Digital

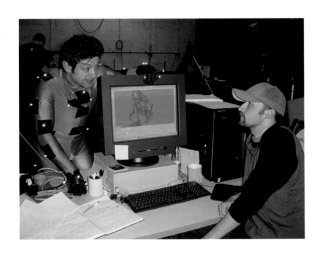

I'm mistaken here, animators don't read 'scripts' as such, they work from storyboards. But here was a dialogue-intensive character with real emotions. Everyone had to be on the same wavelength to make this work.

Animators are actors in the sense that they draw from their own life experience and emotions and bring that to a character. They even use their own facial expressions to convey a feeling by acting into a mirror. However, if there are 40 animators working on individual segments of Gollum, the string that holds the pearls on the necklace, so to speak, could be missing, and given that the character has such a complex psychological and emotional journey, he could take on 40 different personalities! But here there was a very different agenda. Instead of looking into mirrors, the animators would be using the performance of a single actor, and sticking closely to the footage we had shot on location and in motion capture, and that would be the emotional string that would hold it together.

So there was a summit of all Gollum personnel, everyone had a script, and Fran galvanised the entire team so that everyone knew precisely what we were doing. It was a major turning point for Gollum. At last he was really going to impact on the story in a significant and real way.

Peter, Elijah, Sean and I were driven back up to Ohakune to shoot a key new scene, where the division between Frodo and Sam really begins to grow. Sam is mocking Gollum, but Frodo defends him, telling Sam that he wants to save the wretch. Sam thinks that Frodo is being manipulated, and implies that he sounds more and more like Gollum himself. Meanwhile Gollum, unaware of this conversation, is desperately trying to catch a fish. He seems happier now, almost like a child that is being shown affection at last. I wanted there to be a sense of him looking back at Frodo as if to say, 'Look at me, Dad!'

The chosen location for this scene was Mangawherro Falls, under the great Mount Ruapehu. The vista that Peter wanted to shoot was spectacular. However, there was a problem. It was under a deep layer of snow, and it needed to look like summer. I was on standby, waiting in the hotel for my call. Peter decided he wanted to go ahead with the shot, if the snow could be cleared in time, and so the crew got to work with high pressure hoses, heaters and blowtorches, trying to melt the snow and ice that covered the area that was going to be in shot. By lunchtime they'd done it.

I was brought on to set, wearing a wetsuit that felt about three inches thick – I could barely move in it, let alone act as Gollum. The glacial melt water in the stream I would be fishing in was extremely cold, but I thought, *Well, at least the wetsuit will keep me warm.* Wrong! When Pete called action and I dived in, I could hardly breathe it was so cold. I thrashed about inelegantly, mostly trying to stay alive, and – oh yes – trying to act catching a fish. It wasn't very good, so Pete got me to do it again. Four times.

'You tries to choke poor Sméagol'

I stood over a monitor staring at a shot of Gollum that had been animated on top of the motion capture we'd done in the last block. Something wasn't right, and it took me a while to figure it out. Then the penny dropped. They had facially animated to the wrong soundtrack. We had painstakingly re-recorded dialogue over the motion capture sessions for the animators to work from as the

definitive track, and somewhere in the vast machine, they had got lost. The animators never received the sound files. Weeks and weeks of animation work had been done with the wrong vocal tracks.

I was absolutely heartbroken. There was little enough closure on scenes for me as it was, but psychologically I'd signed off on those particular scenes and was moving on. It was now too late to do anything about it, because it had gone too far down the production pipe. Peter, Fran and Barrie were alerted and a full search was launched for the missing files. They had vanished, never to be found. I would eventually re-record these scenes over a year later. There weren't many days I went under but that day was one of them.

World Cup 2002 fever gripped us during the reshoots. Dave Williams and Nigel Nally were our very capable social secretaries. Every night after filming, a designated bar, house or hotel room became a venue for the obligatory screaming-at-television sessions, followed by ferocious late-night analysis and the diminishing of Wellington's beer supplies.

So how on earth Sean Astin managed to drag an entire crew out on a horrendously wet Sunday morning, after weeks of filming and a big Saturday night out, to help him shoot his short film, I will never know. *The Long and the Short of It*, is a prime example of the *Rings* family being there for each other, through thick and through thin. Sean can charm the pants off your butt, and he did, God love him. It was actually great fun, in that sort of masochistic, 'I can hardly stand up because my veins are still flowing with pure alcohol' way. We all took on different roles to what we normally did – for instance Andrew Lesnie, our distinguished director of photography), played the starring role as 'the grizzly painter' (rather touchingly I might add); Mr Peter Jackson played a bus driver, proving once again that cameo performances can steal a movie; Mark Ordesky stepped down from executive producer to be coffee boy; Elijah Wood assumed command as first assistant director, and I was promoted from being man covered in dots; to man with traffic cones – except I had a cunning plan and elbowed my way into being producer by lunchtime. Then I worked my way back down the ladder by teatime. The film is really excellent and is featured on the *The Two Towers* DVD, with more information online at www.seanastin.com.

When I received the pages for the central schizophrenic scene, I was buzzing. It was a full-on internal debate in which Sméagol emerges and admits his growing allegiance to his new master, Frodo, for which Gollum utterly castigates him. Fran had supremely crafted a journey right into the psyche and guts of Gollum/Sméagol. I instantly recognised that this was a key scene and that it would be the moment when the audience would either get into his head or not. So far they had been kept at arm's length, with only little clues as to whom this character really was.

When the day came to shoot it, I was ready to take it on.

We shot the whole scene in single takes, which last around three minutes or so, so that the dynamic of the relationship of these two distinct personalities could bounce off each other. It was like being back on stage performing a monologue. Fran gave exquisite notes and between us we found the shifts in tone throughout the scene. Once we were happy with the master shot, we then concentrated on the individual development of each personality. Gollum became more cruel and Sméagol became more downtrodden until the crucial turning point in the scene when Gollum calls Sméagol a murderer, at which point he's pushed him too far. From here on in Sméagol's courage grows and Gollum becomes more and more desperate, eventually losing his grip. Sméagol, momentarily, is free.

The following day, we shot the same scene on the motion capture stage. Not having a year between shooting on set and on the mocap stage was such joy!

Out of all the Gollum/Sméagol scenes in

the trilogy, this is the one I'm most proud of.

Fran and Peter had decided that Sméagol's murder of Déagol was so dark that it would be impossible for the audience to sympathise with him at all, so they wanted reshoot some of the fight to make it less one-sided, as if Déagol could just as easily have been affected by the Ring and would defend his right to it strongly.

I had said that, if possible, I wanted to avoid my frontal lobotomy haircut this time, as I'd be getting married in a couple of weeks, so Gino very kindly prepared a bald cap to go over the hairline, under the wig.

It was great to see Thomas again. When we got up to the location at Shelly Bay, the wind was ferocious. Fran directed a shot in which Sméagol and Déagol fight, then Déagol falls backwards and smashes his head on a rock. We then see a moment of remorse in Sméagol's face before the lure of the Ring takes over and he falls under its spell.

A huge transparent canopy had been erected so that we could work on if it rained. We battled on in the rain and wind for as long as we could, until a gale blew under the canopy, lifting the front end of a camera

Pick-Ups: Frodo, Sam, Gollum, Faramir - 13 May 2002

313.87 EXT. FIRST CAMP, ITHILIEN - NIGHT (NEW SCENE)
NIGHT has fallen. FRODO and SAM are SLEEPING. GOLLUM is awake and agitated. He is engaged in an INTERNAL DEBATE.

SMEAGOL: What does they want with Mordor? Why does Master want to go there?

GOLLUM: We doesn't know... but they're hiding something from us, Precious. Sneaky little Hobbitses! Wicked! Tricky! False!

SMEAGOL: No...

GOLLUM: Yes, Precious - false. They will cheat you, hurt you! Lie!

SMEAGOL: No! Not master.

GOLLUM: Master!!! Master doesn't like you - Master doesn't care!

SMEAGOL: He does! He does care!

GOLLUM: Master is using you!

SMEAGOL: No! No! He's my friend.

GOLLUM: (laughs)You don't have any friends. Nobody likes you...

SMEAGOL: Not listening - not listening -

GOLLUM: You're a liar and a thief!

SMEAGOL: No!!!!!!

GOLLUM: (low) Murderer!

SMEAGOL: Go away!

GOLLUM: (mocking) Go away ... Ha! Ha! Ha!

SMEAGOL: I hate you ... I hate you ...

GOLLUM: You make us sick ... where would you be without me? Gollum, Gollum!

SMEAGOL: Leave me alone!

GOLLUM: I saved us! It was me! We survived because of me

SMEAGOL LOOKS UP, A NEW LIGHT OF DEFIANCE IN HIS EYES...

SMEAGOL: Not anymore. Master looks after us now.

GOLLUM: (low and dangerous) No ...

GOLLUM: (fierce whisper)Leave now and never come back.

GOLLUM HISSES!!!!

SMEAGOL: (cont'd) (louder) Leave now and never come back!!!

GOLLUM SNARLS!!!!

SMEAGOL: (cont'd)) (shouting) Leave now and never come back!!!!!

SMEAGOL BREAKS INTO A PEAL OF TRIUMPHANT LAUGHTER. HE SHOUTS THE PHRASE OVER AND OVER ...

SMEAGOL: (cont'd)(ecstatic)We told him to go away! And away he goes, Precious!!! Away he goes!!!! Gone! Gone! Gone! Smeagol is free!

department truck, which it had been tied to, off the ground. Barrie wrapped the shoot. It was too dangerous; we'd reconvene in the morning on a set inside.

I was in the make-up chair having my ears stuck on the following morning when I was asked to go and see Peter. This was unusual, but off I went. Peter told me that Fran was unwell, and was unable to work today. He asked me if I'd direct the scene, with director of photography Richard Bluck, who had shot a lot of the Gollum scenes, taking care of the camera side of things. We'd shoot some stuff and then we'd bring it over on a clamshell (handheld video player) for Pete to look at.

Overnight Dan Hennah, Alan Lee and the art department had rebuilt the entire set in a studio. It was extraordinary. It was as if they had lifted up this huge area of land and put it down again in one piece. I'll never understand how they do it.

So Thomas and I talked about the scene, and then we played the moment of Sméagol and Déagol's fight for possession of the Ring like two schoolboys in a playground scrap that turns nasty, both of them losing control and finding themselves in a bloody fight to the death. It seemed to work, and it gave the Ring a greater role in the scene too. It was vicious, and we both went for it.

It was a real challenge directing and acting at the same time, I'd never done it before, but I knew the character so well by now, it was not a problem.

My favourite shot was tracking along as Sméagol runs and jumps on Déagol's back. They fall to the ground and the Ring falls out of his hand. The huge Ring lies in the foreground with these two bodies in the mid-distance fighting away, unaware of the power that's driving them.

The work that the animators had been doing on Gollum was beautiful. It was such a thrill watching him grow into this amazingly real, textured creature. The detail in the eyes was remarkable. They were so translucent and reflected light so truthfully, they really were now the window to his soul. The skin and teeth, and even the hair (which had always presented them with problems, finding a way to create natural movement) were now all looking so real. And what they'd been doing with the raw material of my performance on set and in motion capture was so inspiring. They were managing to capture the essence of what I was doing and then augment it, taking it to another level, amplifying the underlying psychology of the acting with their phenomenal talent. The number of Gollum shots had increased dramatically and yet everyone was rising to the challenge. We were really feeding off each other now.

The defining moment for me of the Gollum motion capture was the soliloquy of Sméagol /Gollum. With the simple act of turning his head Andy changed between characters so completely it was awe-inspiring. Not to mention hair-raising! And he did this for several takes in a row, seemingly without effort. Nowhere in the movie were Sméagol and Gollum so well defined, in my opinion. Although this motion capture was not used in the end, with Peter deciding on animation for this scene, it was wonderful to have been able to witness it in real-time.

Mahria Sangster,
Mocap Co-ordinator, S/G BIT

A thing I've always really appreciated about Peter is that he will stick with something until he's satisfied he's got it. And apparently he didn't think he had really solved to his satisfaction the problem of presenting the split personality of Gollum in a way that would be clear to the audience until he came up with the split personality sequence in The Two Towers. *The finished scene is like a great aria, and is cleverly directed — he's muttering back and forth between himself, but the way it's shot it's seemingly two characters, one talking to the other. It's just a matter of camera angle, and the way Pete did it was so simple that the audience immediately got it, so it's perfect.*

Randall William Cook, Animation Design Supervisor

The day came when the first, defining Gollum 'shot' had been completed. It was amazing. It became a new benchmark and everybody was excited. Beth had been working on the shot of Sméagol at the Forbidden Pool, the moment of slight distrust when Frodo has called him, and for a second he senses something's not right, before he says, 'We must go... now?' She had cracked it. She had caught incredibly subtle nuances in the tension between the passivity of his gaze and the slight unease of his breath. It was beautiful to look at and is one of my favourite shots in the whole of *The Two Towers*.

Buck called me over. 'Andy, can you come over here a second? I got this shot and I wanna get it approved by PJ and Fran. It's the bit where you go, "Isweedan", and Sméagol's kinda rockin', and I'm not sure what the hell you're doin' buddy.'

'Isweedan'? What the hell is 'Isweedan'? I thought to myself. I had no idea what he was talking about. So, I bowled over to his computer and he showed me. When I saw the shot, I couldn't stop laughing. Now this is an example of the pressures the animators were working under. The scene had been edited and Buck had been given his piece of the shot to work on. However the dialogue had been chopped up. The section in question was the at Forbidden Pool where Sméagol is singing, 'the rock and pool, *is sweet and cool.*' Poor old Buck only had the bit 'is sweet an...', a shot that lasts a couple of seconds, which was understandably completely unfathomable out of context.

Motion capture and working with the animators had finally reached an end for *The Two Towers*, however ADR – the definitive vocal performance – had yet to be completed. It was a really bizarre situation,

because every scene had shots that were at completely different stages of development, so having a coherent picture to record voice to was impossible. Up on screen, there would be a few frames of me giving my on set performance, then a few frames of motion capture CG Gollum, then a few frames of a wire frame Gollum over my performance, then a few frames of a fully rendered, skinned and lit Gollum. It was very disconcerting, and those were the easy scenes

Andy Serkis is not just a very good actor, but also a mountaineer, a very physical guy, and very active. We tried to use him as a basis for all the motion and then apply the artistry of the digital animators who could work in concert with that, making it an ensemble character. I also tried to get them to look at other aspects of Gollum a little more: all the Olivier and Orson Welles Shakespearean stuff, I even got some footage of John Barrymore doing Richard III. *What I was trying to do was show real acting, human beings, because that's what they were emulating. I also went into stage etiquette with them, things we didn't want Gollum to do — upstaging, or picking his nose while Frodo is delivering an important bit of information — because it's not polite to a fellow actor.*

I guess I saw it as trying to create an actor inside the computer. That was difficult because Gollum was this collaborative creation, spread across a number of people coming at it from different directions and motivations depending on their department's input, but we were all aiming at the same thing and I think we got there. The physical contortions that Andy would undergo to connote Gollum on stage did not necessarily translate to the digital Gollum with the same impact. As a result, we had to find a way to get his essence there — there were times when Andy couldn't crawl face-first down a cliff, make a leap across a room, any number of things Gollum was compelled to do — so we had to speculate after Andy gave us the start of a movement and the finish, leaving us to the fill the gap between.

Randall William Cook, *Animation Design Supervisor*

– then you had all those permutations with Gollum *and* Sméagol! Finally time had run out and we were going to have to resume in London when Peter and Fran came over to record the score with Howard. It was going to go to the wire.

22 July 2002

Lorraine and I got married in a twelfth century Romanesque church, 20km south of Florence, and the festivities were held in a castle near Fiesole, in the hills overlooking Tuscany. It was the most fantastic day. Over a hundred of our friends and family had flown over and we all stayed in villas near Gréve in the Chianti region. The partying went on for days. It totally exceeded our expectations.

We didn't want it to end, but rather appropriately our 'honeymoon' was actually

to be a rehearsal room at the Royal Exchange Theatre in Manchester, where we had met 13 years previously and where we were about to start rehearsing *Othello*, directed by Braham Murray. I would be playing Iago, with Lorraine as his wife Emelia.

In Shakespeare's most brilliantly intense

When I first began working at Weta Digital, my role was focused on character rigging, which is the technique for setting up animation controls that allow animators to manipulate the characters. You can liken it to building the wood and strings on a marionette – controls (the rig) are built in the computer that allow animators to grab arms, wrists, legs, hips, etc. and manipulate them into a particular pose. By having Gollum as the main focus, it allowed us to aim for an extremely high level of control, which we could then trickle down into the other creatures (the Balrog, Cave Troll, digital doubles, etc.).

While I certainly enjoyed rigging the characters, my goal had always been to animate. I would watch Randy Cook doing tests with the Cave Troll, making him run around, swinging his arms, and all I could think was Iwannadothat Iwannadothat Iwannadothat! While working on Gollum, I decided that the best way to test the rig was to actually try animating something. So one Saturday, I came into work, grabbed a large cup of coffee, and tried to come up with something interesting to animate. I ended up doing a quick animation of Gollum leaping up on to a Gandalf model, ripping its head off, tossing the head to the ground, and then leaping on to the now dismembered cranium, rolling off screen with it. On the Monday I showed the animation to Randy, not quite sure what to expect. He watched it cycle through a few times and then said (and I'll always remember this), 'So, what, you want to animate on this picture?' I think I squeaked out a measly 'Yes please'.

Jason Schleifer, Creature Designer, Weta Digital

domestic tragedy, Othello the General falls in love with Desdemona, and 'honest' Iago, his closest friend and sergeant major, cannot bear it and plots his destruction. Playing Iago and Gollum at the same time is bad for your mental health. It means you are constantly full of hatred. I began to draw comparisons between the characters. There are a million theories as to Iago's motivations, but I believed that Iago was once a good soldier, a great man's man to have around, a bit of a laugh, who feels betrayed, gets jealous of his friend, wants to mess it up for him, enjoys causing him pain, makes a choice to channel all his creative energy into the destruction of this human being, and becomes completely addicted to the power he wields over him. I didn't want to play him as initially malevolent. He's not the devil. He's you or me feeling jealous and not being able to control our feelings. We may want to destroy someone in our minds, fantasize about how, but most of us don't actually do it. Iago, like Gollum, cannot help himself, and like Gollum elicits a sympathy from the audience, who know they should hate him but they cannot help liking him. Iago manages to thrill the audience so much with his scheming that they almost want him to succeed. They are then forced to question their own morality.

Iago is the largest role in the entire Shakespearean cannon. The pressure was on. But the final voice tracks for Gollum also had to be completed, the culmination of all the work I'd done so far, so every weekend throughout rehearsals, I'd travel from Manchester to London to record Gollum. I really felt as if my brain was going to explode, particularly on the final session at Pinewood Studios where we frantically recorded Gollum for 14 hours straight because we were out of time, then I went straight back to Manchester. I thought I'd never manage it.

Rehearsals were getting more and more intense, and the relationship between Othello and Iago more and more electric. And then, just as we were about to open the play, and I was beginning to relish playing the role, I had a stroke of bad luck, injuring my lower back. I tried to convince myself it was nothing and, desperate to get through the opening, took painkillers and got on with it. They did the trick, the production opened and was highly critically acclaimed.

I managed to get through 40 performances, but with each one it became more and more difficult to mask the pain, until one matinee I passed out on stage in front of 750 people. I knew I was in trouble. Leaving the production was heartbreaking and traumatic for all concerned, and I spent three weeks unable to move a muscle. Backs are a nightmare. There are more theories about backs than Iago's motives, but I was eventually saved by two people, an acupuncturist called Joshua Enkin and a physiotherapist called Kevin Lidlow. If it wasn't for them, I would never have been able to fly out to New York for the world premiere of *The Two Towers.*

CHAPTER TWELVE
The Two Towers

Every night in the weeks leading up to the opening of *The Two Towers* I woke up terribly anxious and totally wired, running and re-running the scenes in my head. I worried for Gollum.

I'm beginning to feel like it's time for my young child to go to school for the first time, while I stand at the gates and wave goodbye, and watch him mingle into the crowds.

The plane touched down in New York, and I was driven directly to a private screening room, where I was going to see *The Two Towers* for the first time. It was just great to see Mark Ordesky, who (along with Barrie, Peter, Fran and everybody else) had survived the most phenomenally taxing year. His smile seemed to read, 'Well, we've done it, dunno how... but we did!' Other cast members who hadn't seen it yet, Bernard Hill (Théoden), Miranda Otto (Eowyn) and Karl Urban (Éomer), were also there.

As the lights went down, my heart started thumping and my eyes started burning, I really thought I was going to be sick. I felt like I was in a car crash, everything in slooow mooootion. Each frame flickering by one by one, every twenty-fourth of a second Gollum was on screen, I felt as naked as him... and then the three hours were gone!

I just didn't know what had happened. I mean, I knew I'd been blown away by the whole film, but what was Gollum like? I wanted to see it again immediately, but I would have to wait a few days until the premiere. First we had to meet the press.

During the build-up to the opening, another build-up was happening in the world– the build-up to war in Iraq, a war on terror. Some of the press who had seen *The Two Towers* drew analogies between the film and world events. In the cast we all had differing opinions. I personally believe that Tolkien wrote a complex universal story and Peter Jackson had made a complex universal feature film. The audience will draw from the storytelling according to their world view, but the darkness in the film certainly resonated for me.

Now I'd done press for lots of films before, but nothing could prepare me for the sheer volume of journalists from all media that were there to dissect and spread the word on *The Two Towers*. Fortunately, I had a great deal of help from Marcel Pariseau, my newly engaged publicist, who showed me the ropes. For days on end you sit in a chair, in a hotel room, in front of a backdrop of the film's poster with lights and cameras set up, and answer, 70 TV interviewers a day in three-minute soundbites. THE SAME QUESTIONS! It's like *Groundhog Day*.

Gollum had made quite an impact at the press screenings, and journalists were talking about 'his' performance as if he was real, not a CG character at all. So when they came in to interview me, they were fascinated to learn about the process. They weren't sure if he was animated or if he was an actor in make-up. All they knew was that they'd connected with him in some way. I had a bit of an uphill struggle at first, because I had a lot of information to get over in a short space of

time. It wasn't as simple as just talking about the character I'd played. This is a sample of how the early interviews went:

Reporter: *So you did the voice of Gollum, right?*
Andy: *Well, yeah but it wasn't just the voi—*
Reporter: *But they must have treated it in post-production? I mean you don't sound anything like him.*
Andy: *Well actually, no, but can I just go back to the first question, erm, I did the movement as well, because we shot every thing on set and then—*
Reporter (amazed): *You mean you actually went down to New Zealand to do this?*
Andy (already feeling homicidal): *Yes! And I originally acted the scenes during principal photography with Elijah and Sean so that—*
Reporter: *Amazing! Wow, I thought you just did the voice on top of the animation in a studio in London or—*

Andy: *No, no, I played Gollum on set. You know, crawling around, doing the voice, acting with Elijah and Sean.*
Reporter: *Right, so you were a kind of stand in and was that useful for Elijah and Sean?*

And this was before I could even start explaining the finer points of motion capture, rotoscoping, key-frame animation and all the technical processes, and the collaboration with everyone involved with bringing Gollum to life. It was quite a stressful time, being under that amount of media scrutiny, and so I was quite relieved when we finally reached the opening night and the public could see it for themselves and make up their own minds.

It was a very special night, Lorraine had flown over, together with my close friends Bev, Jo and Lee. It was brilliant to have them there to share it with, and we all chuckled away at the fact that here we all were, in a stretch limo, driving through a snow-covered

New York City, to the world premiere of *The Lord of the Rings: The Two Towers*.

Suddenly the door opened, and we'd arrived at the theatre. As we all climbed out, on to the red carpet crammed with photographers and TV crews, I thought to myself, *No one is going to recognise me because Gollum is CG, short, bald, and let's face it, pretty unattractive, oh well...* But as soon as my feet hit the carpet, some *Rings* fans started shouting, 'ANDY!' and I could see the photographers thinking, *Who is this guy?* Then Marcel announced, 'This is Andy Serkis who plays Gollum'. The flashguns started to go off and it felt very surreal, as if I were in a very strange movie where I'm playing an actor going to the first night of a movie.

Inside the auditorium, the lights went down, and Peter walked into a centre-stage spotlight for the second year in a row. The roars of support were deafening. He introduced the cast and personnel who were present and we all came up on stage one by one. When the opening titles and theme began to play, I could feel the hairs standing up on the back of my neck. The audience cheered, their wait was over, and the film began...

I was obviously highly sensitised to Gollum's every appearance, not least because Lorraine was holding my hand so tight I have permanent nails marks in my palms, but when we reached the first big schizophrenic monologue scene, where Sméagol banishes Gollum, the audience's reaction slowly turned from laughter to a real, tangible feeling of sympathy, and you could hear a pin drop. This was Gollum's defining moment, which everyone had spent all those thousands of hours of creative energy working towards in the quest to make him real.

After New York, I went to the premieres in Paris, London and Los Angeles, but I skipped Wellington, where an enormous Gollum, courtesy of Weta Workshop, dominated the Embassy Theatre.

Is Gollum Oscar-worthy?

Actors' performances (beyond just the voice) being used in animation is not new. It's as old as the Hollywood hills. Disney's animators had literally traced over actors to give them a greater reality. Hans Conried, the actor who played Captain Hook in *Peter Pan,* gave a complete performance in costume, which was used as reference, as did Adriana Caselotti, the actress who played Snow White. In *Who Framed Roger Rabbit?* Bob Hoskins had an actor dressed in a rabbit suit on set for him to play off, and in the new *Star Wars* films, Ahmed Best, who played Jar-Jar Binks, was on set acting with Ewan McGregor and Liam Neeson.

But what we had achieved collectively was taking a great character from literature, filtering that character through great screenwriters, then taken the emotion, physicality and voice of an actor's performance, which had organically grown from acting with other actors on set, and synthesised it with a range of animation techniques and motion capture. This was then rendered inside a skin so real it looked like you could touch it, and then meticulously lit and comped back into original environments so that he unquestionably existed as a real being and that the audience was allowed to feel a connection with this hideous-looking creature rather than just being impressed with technical magic.

I was asked by New Line Cinema to return to Los Angeles after Christmas to promote their ambition for a supporting actor Oscar nomination bid. I arrived in LA and immediately began the rounds of satellite television, radio and print interviews.

It became necessary to find an analogy for the actor/digital/animation relationship to succinctly put across how Gollum had been achieved. I had made references to the fact that me playing Gollum was no different from an acting point of view, to, say, someone like John Rhys Davies playing Gimli, in the sense that he wears prosthetics created by a team of artists, and is therefore completely unrecognisable, but his performance is driven by an actor. When the talk of potential nomination bids came up, it was mentioned that John Hurt had been nominated for best supporting actor for *The Elephant Man*, an example of an actor's performance enhanced by a team of prosthetic make-up artists.

This was to cause a heated debate in Hollywood and in the worldwide film-making and animation communities. Critics were soon asking, where does an actor's performance end and 'enhancement' begin? And this grey area would lay down the gauntlet to many award-giving bodies that would have to sit up and take notice of this new type of hybrid performance.

Peter and Weta Digital, along with New Line, cut together an amazing piece of footage which demonstrated the synthesis of acting performance with animation, showing side by side my face and the fully animated Gollum face in the central schizophrenic scene, which was so much more eloquent than any amount of explaining I tried to do.

I also made public appearances at the Arclight Cinema on Hollywood Boulevard and had a great evening talking to members of the Screen Actors Guild. They had concerns relating to the way Gollum had been achieved. Having now proved that a CG character worked emotionally in a live action feature film, they were worried that a precedent had been set – that actors would be replaced in the long term. I tried to allay their fears, explaining that in fact there were more actor hours spent working on Gollum than on any conventional screen character.

Gollum was really beginning to find his way into the public consciousness. People were going around saying that things were 'precious'! In the intermission of the Superbowl football game there was a fantastic

Saturday Night Live spoof of Gollum/ Sméagol speculating the outcome, and he even appeared briefly in *The Simpsons* episode 'Dude, Where's My Ranch?'

Awards season had come around and the visual effects team were justly rewarded by many award-giving bodies, including the BAFTAs, for their amazing work on *The Two Towers,* and then it was time for the Oscars, which Lorraine and I attended.

Days before the ceremony, US and British forces began to bomb Iraq. Nobody could quite relax and enjoy the festivities. The war was on everybody's mind. Some showed their feelings, some hid them, but we'd gone to support *The Two Towers*, and were delighted that it succeeded in winning two awards, best visual effects, and best sound-editing.

I had no idea we would be working on such a star. Had I known Gollum would be received with so much applause, the task of bringing him to life would probably have seemed all the more daunting. It's rare that one gets the opportunity to work on a character which is on the one hand pathetic and over the top, while, subtly twisted and vindictive on the other. His is the story of how a good soul became corrupted and obsessed. He's a fascinating illustration of how any person can be overcome by their darker seld.

The most common animation comment I received was, 'Make him more intense!'. But his controls were already pushed to the max. It was only after I saw him on screen, in his entirety, that I understood why we had to really bring out the menace, as well as the charm, in Gollum.

Mike Stevens, Creature Designer, Weta Digital

CHAPTER THIRTEEN
The Return of the King

Following the press tour for the *The Two Towers*, I was home for one week in April 2003 and then found myself back on a plane to New Zealand. The 28-hour flight was now a matter of course; however, arriving at Bangkok was slightly disturbing. You get off the plane while it refuels and frantically stretch your dehydrated body to avoid getting deep vein thrombosis and are faced with practically everyone in the airport with masks on trying to avoid the risk of contracting SARS. It slightly freaked me out and I tried to hold my breath for an hour before bolting back on to plane.

I pulled out my battered old copy of *The Lord of the Rings* to re-read the Cirith Ungol chapter, and suddenly one of the air stewardess tapped me on the shoulder.

'Have you seen the films?' she asked, handing me a hot towel. Resisting the temptation to burst out of my seat, crawl on all fours and rasp, 'Yes, precioussss!' I nodded politely as she leant in and conspiratorially boasted, 'You'll never guess who we had on the flight the other day.'

'Who?' I replied. She whispered seductively, 'The good-looking one with the long blond hair... Whatsisname?' I shrugged innocently.

Touching down in Wellington was like seeing a dear friend again, and I got very excited at the prospect of seeing 'the family' and working on the final leg of Gollum's journey. Janine picked me up and whisked me down to Stone Street studios where they had already started reshoots with 'the blond good-looking one', and as I tiptoed on to the

set during a take, it was incredible. It looked as if nobody had moved from where they were standing a year ago, like the stone statues in Narnia. There were lots of silent hugs and kisses and 'How are you?'s as the camera rolled.

And then I saw Billy and Katie Jackson, sitting in their dad's directing chair, looking so grown up, and it really hit me how long this whole thing has taken. Pete called cut, and we gave each other a huge hug and tried to remember how much younger each of our children were when it all began. 'How old's Ruby now?' 'Nearly five, and Sonny's almost three, he wasn't even born...'

I had a day of recovery and catching up with everyone at Weta, seeing all the animators and marvelling at all the cool work they were doing for *The Return of the King*. Some great Gollum shots were already underway, particularly Gollum plotting the Hobbits' fate with Shelob, reflected in a pool. Gino had done some incredible paint schemes for Shelob, and also the battered

Gollum look for the final section on Mount Doom, cut to shreds and showing all the wear and tear of moving through such a hostile environment.

Friday 11 April was to be one of those defining moments in Gollum's journey. I went round to Pete's house to work on the script with Fran and Philippa. It was great to see them after such a long time and we caught up on life since that mad day of ADR at Pinewood last summer. What they had in store for me, and Gollum, completely blew me away. It really brought home to me what incredibly adventurous, fearless screenwriters they were.

Fran had this idea that instead of repeating what we had established in *The Two Towers* – Gollum being the vicious dark side, the survivor, full of hatred and revenge, with the re-emerging Sméagol as the chink of light in his soul, the abused child, the victim who really trusted Frodo, and the side we all felt pity for – that we turn it all on its head so that Sméagol was really the cold, calculating, passive-aggressive psychopath who play acted being the victim to get his own way. In comparison, Gollum would be less dangerous because his passion, lust and aggression were true hot-blooded emotions, flooded with feeling. The idea sent me reeling but I knew instinctively that this would be the way to go, that the character would deepen and take the audience on a very complex journey.

My only worries were, I suppose, that it questioned my world view. I had played Gollum as someone who, at the end of the day, no matter what he'd done, was a very sick addict and was redeemable because he was the victim of a powerful force that he couldn't handle; the message for the audience was Gandalf's 'be careful how you hand out judgement'. Now we were looking at a character who is pure evil, past all redemption. My brain was frazzled by the implications and, still jet-lagged, I was unable to sleep because my mind was racing.

On Saturday morning I went into the motion capture stage to test out the new Gollum 'charmap' (new software which has updated the look of the CG puppet) in preparation for shooting, on Monday. It was amazing to see how the place had evolved. There was even a proper roof now, which meant that the banks of computers didn't have to be covered with umbrellas every time it rained. And there were 52 cameras now, almost double, giving a larger area to work in with a higher resolution, picking up finer detail of movement. It was great to see all the guys – Lisa, Frank and Moggey were there to greet me, along with the new mocap consultant, David Bawel.

And there it was, hanging up and ready for action, my lovely blue Lycra suit. As soon as I slipped it on, I realised how much I'd missed it. Believe me it was... emotional. (The night before was Orlando Bloom's last shot on the film, and he was given a tremendous send off, with the stunt guys performing the *haka* and Pete presenting him with Legolas' bow as a very special memento of his time on the films. Afterwards, Pete came up to me and said, 'Of course, Andy, when you do *your* final shot, I shall have to present you with the blue suit.')

Anyway, as I stood in the middle of the mocap stage assuming the familiar 'T' pose and heard Moggey give his 'OK, you're live', I thought to myself, *Here we go again*, and down I went on all fours and back into Gollum's head and body as if I'd never left it.

Because of the difference in my body's shape and Gollum's, there are certain adjustments I'd had to make. One of these had always been a bit of a problem and this time round we wanted to sort it out – if I put my hand to my face, what you see on screen is Gollum's hand passing through his head. The distances don't correlate, so I always had to compensate by imagining I'm putting my hand to my face when really it's about six inches in front of it. When I'm in character, I don't really want to have to think about that, so David and Moggey had spent time adjusting the curvature of the spine on the Gollum puppet, so that his hand movement matched mine.

On Monday we shot the Cirith Ungol scene, in which Gollum begins poisoning Frodo against Sam, using his wiles to convince him that Sam has no understanding of what it's like to bear the Ring and that only Sméagol will look after his master. It was a real technical challenge, and it took me a while to hit my stride.

Fran and Philippa have written the most amazing scene for the flashback sequence of Sméagol killing Déagol for the Ring. Sméagol is really becoming the devious, self-possessed child who has to be managed by Gollum. The addiction to the Ring makes them powerless to resist, but Sméagol has a secret agenda, to keep it for himself. We shot 22 takes of this scene, playing out different variations, looking at the different levels of real tragic self-pity against the comedic potential of Gollum trying to keep Sméagol focused on the job of leading the Hobbits to Shelob.

Gollum's final moment

This was one of the most difficult days of filming I have had on this movie. We were shooting the scene in which Gollum, after he's finally got the Ring, falls into the Crack of Doom. Randy had mapped out a previz shot (a basic animated sketch of how it might possibly look), which had Gollum scrabbling to get the Ring as he falls through the air, managing to catch it, and then holding it to his chest, before plunging into the molten lava. We all discussed what the final moment should be, how the audience should receive the death of this character, and also, and perhaps more importantly, the end of the Ring.

As I lay down flat on a padded rig, so that they could shoot motion capture and live reference from above, I thought to myself *How is it possible to play this without being melodramatic?* It's such an epic moment, and yet within it, the human reality of falling to one's death had to play truthfully. It was really a matter of just going for it and seeing what came out, which I have to say felt pretty awful! It was the direction that came from Fran, Philippa and Randy, that helped me through. Death scenes are always hellishly difficult to play, but this one was the mother of all death scenes, and I really don't know if I pulled off my side of the bargain.

Winning a Saturn Award from the Academy of Science Fiction, Fantasy and Horror was the first time the acting contribution to the role had been recognised formally, and this for me was thrilling. It symbolised a growing understanding and respect for the craft of acting in a new realm.

A week later Gollum wasawarded an MTV award for a new category ' best virtual performance'. I recorded an acceptance speech in New Zealand, thanking MTV, on behalf of all those who worked on him, when all of a sudden Gollum himself burst in, ripped the award out of my hands and started to verbally attack everyone, claiming that it was his award, and his only.

June 2003

Back for final reshoots, new scenes and motion capture... one... last... time.

I'm staying in a fabulous old wooden house in Breaker Bay, right next to the ocean.

From a rocky promontory along the beach you can see the snow-capped mountains of Kaikoura on the South Island. Summer at home, winter here. It's beautiful. Last night Philippa had a dinner party and a lot of the cast were there. There's a kind of sadness creeping in, that get-togethers like this on such a regular basis will soon be a thing of the past.

But not yet, there's work to be done. Stone Street Studios are full on. There's not a scrap of space on the lot that hasn't got a set built on it. Three construction crews are working round the clock to build these masterpieces, then we arrive and shoot on them, then they rip them down ready for the next one to take its place.

And the next piece of the jigsaw in the ever-evolving motion capture puzzle will be shooting motion capture on the real set *at the same time as shooting on film with the other actors!* In true Peter Jackson style, there's no letting up in the last leg of the race, he's still trying to push technical boundaries, experiment, develop. Wow, I can't wait for this. If this works, then all the energy created between the actors will be harnessed simultaneously on celluloid *and* in pixels! It'll be fascinating

to see how computer world crew and camera world crew co-exist on the same set. At the moment they have different, rhythms and languages, they are different tribes with different customs.

The first time motion capture is used on set works like a dream. There are no technical hitches, and nothing is held up. In a way I'm really glad it didn't happen like that originally because a lot of experimentation went into Gollum's character during those years of doing it the old way. But now it speeds up the whole process and will be so much easier for all the departments to assemble the shots and for Peter to cut the scenes. I am delighted for all my friends in the mocap team – years of hard work has brought them to this point. They are clearly delighted with the success of the day.

Finally we come full circle. Scene 558 is back. Peter and Fran have decided to re-shoot one of the first days of filming I ever did: the big confrontation between Gollum, Sam and Frodo on the upper slopes of Mount Doom. It's so much better now, so much more

Animating Gollum was all about method acting in reverse. Instead of studying a 500-year-old junkie Hobbit and getting into character, I found that a 500-year-old junkie Hobbit was studying me, and taking over my life. For about six months we walked, talked, ate and slept Gollum. The effect on our mental and physical well-being was extreme. Some of us are now initiating court proceedings against New Line to demand restorative surgery. I for one would like to get rid of the globular eyes and the tendency to gulp!

Mary Victoria,
Creature Designer, Weta Digital

dramatic. And the journeys for all of our characters have developed hugely over the years. The tension that has built up between Gollum and Sam reaches boiling point and the fight is now really strongly motivated and consequently more brutal. The momentary triumph that Gollum has over Frodo is so twisted and cruel.

It's getting sad now. As each day goes by, another member of the cast has their final day on set and is given a wonderful farewell. Last night was Viggo Mortensen's (Aragorn), which was amazing. He is so respected by everyone, and his departure was very moving. Next to go is Ian McKellen, then Sean, then Dom and Billy, and then next week it will be Elijah and me. I will still have some more motion capture and ADR, and then it'll be farewell New Zealand until December when we'll all get back together here in Wellington, for the world premiere of *The Return of the King.*

The world is changing...
I can feel it in the pixels

In the film industry, people have suddenly woken up to the potential of working with motion or performance capture. Directors, producers and actors like Tom Hanks and Robert Zemeckis are taking on CGI projects such as *Polar Express,* and it seems that a brave new world is opening up that at last uses evolving technology not to celebrate itself and to dominate the artistry, but to let the artistry lead the way.

Cinema is as much about the evolution of technology as it is storytelling, but for a time, effects driven movies often lacked humanity, and so there is movement towards putting the balance back. Peter Jackson's vision, ability to push boundaries and commitment to honest storytelling with emotionally involving characters will, in my opinion, inspire a sea-change in film-making.

It's a very exciting time for actors, too. Performance capture will be used more and more, but the technology will become less and less invasive, allowing acting to retain its purity. As I have discovered, it does require pure, truthful acting – no costume, no set, no make-up – but offers the potential of an infinite range of characters that can be literally mapped on to an actor's interpretation of a role.

When we were shooting on the motion capture stage for *The Two Towers*, a number of 'industry' people visited the set, and several said to me, 'Hey Andy, this is like watching cinema history being made.' I would politely agree, then crawl back on to a rock ready for the next take and think nothing of it. But since *The Two Towers* was released and witnessing the film community's response, I suppose I do feel that we have collectively pioneered this new way of integrating acting with animation and digital technology, and that is very rewarding. Remington Scott, the motion capture supervisor on *The Two Towers*, refers to it as 'acting for the twenty-first century', and yet it also feels strangely close to the older acting arenas of theatre, puppetry and plain old sitting round a campfire, telling stories.

For the DVD release of The Fellowship of the Ring *we briefly discussed the possibility of removing the Mark One Gollum and inserting our new Andy Serkis Mark Two version, but as it turned out, we were so frantically busy with getting* The Two Towers *shots done that we didn't have time to put it in the schedule. But it is conceivable that if there's a boxset DVD in a few years' time that we might go back and replace those shots. The trouble is, once you start doing that, the CG technology will have advanced, and Weta Digital will want to replace every Gollum shot, indeed every FX shot, through the whole trilogy. Perhaps one day we'll go back and do a twenty-fifth anniversary improved edition and re-do every visual effects shot in the entire thing. Who knows what technology will be like then?*

Peter Jackson, Director

The good, the bad... and the precious

'Many that live deserve death. And some that die deserve life. Can you give it to them? Then do not be too eager to deal out death in judgement. For even the very wise cannot see all ends. I have not much hope that Gollum can be cured before he dies, but there is a chance of it. And he is bound up with the fate of the Ring. My heart tells me that he has some part to play yet, for good or ill, before the end.'

Sméagol killed Déagol for the Ring. The consequences of that action changed his life forever, and what pleasure he got from the 'precious' was short lived and soon turned into a personal hell on earth. If Sméagol were alive today in our society, if he were on death row serving a life sentence for a drug-related murder that was committed ten years ago when he was a teenager, I wonder how he would be viewed?

It's so easy to see those sorts of people as monsters, as evil people different from us, and that, in my opinion, is where the danger lies – in taking the moral high ground. That is what Frodo initially wants to do, but Gandalf makes him reserve judgement, enabling Frodo to find pity for Gollum, who does indeed play a role, perhaps inadvertently, in bringing the Ring to its final destination, and thus saving Middle-earth.

What would you do if you had the Ring? Imagine having in your grasp the most potent, powerful object ever created, capable of fulfilling your greatest ambition. Could you have the strength to destroy it? Would you try to tame it? Would you try to use it to get what you wanted, or would you try to use it as a means to achieve a goal for your family or country? These, of course, are some of the great themes of *The Lord of the Rings* books, and that's why Tolkien refuses to be pinned down to specific moments in history. I believe he, like many great authors, gives moral responsibility to the reader, and lays the challenge of answering the question at their feet.

Hopefully, what I've tried to do as an actor delivering a performance for an audience, is in tune with Tolkien's philosophy that asking moral questions is far more useful, interesting and, let's face it, entertaining than saying, *I can give you all the answers.*

One of the most unexpected observations I've made about myself, working on this character for such a long time, is that initially I thought I was playing such an extreme creature who was so far removed from who I am that I could happily relish hiding behind the 'characterisation' – the voice and the way he moves physically. In fact, as the process developed, I think, bizarrely, that there is more of myself in this role than any other role I've ever played, even considering that for the majority of the time I'm transmuted into pixels.

This film-making experience has been life-changing in many ways. As an actor, you

rarely get to work on a film when you work and live with fellow cast and crew members in a caring and highly creative environment, over such a long period of time; you rarely get to work in one of the most beautiful countries in the world, populated with genuinely lovely people and you rarely get to work with screenwriters of great integrity and a director of genius. The filming of *The Lord of the Rings* trilogy represented all of these things.

So that's it. I've confessed all the inner workings of this warped cyber-thespian's mind, and the time has come to put away the file on Gollum so that I can make room in my head for a future creature of the imagination.